For the LOVE of Cats

AMY D. SHOJAI AND IRENE GIZZI

PUBLICATIONS INTERNATIONAL, LTD.

CONTRIBUTING WRITERS:

Amy D. Shojai is a contributing editor for *Cat Fancy* and *Cats* Magazine. She is the founder and president of the International Cat Writers' Association, Inc. A former veterinary technician, she is the author of several pet books including *The Cat Companion* and *The Incomparable Cat*.

Irene Gizzi is a former vice president and current member of the American Cat Association. She has been a licensed all breed cat judge and cat breeder for over twenty years. She has written numerous cat and pet columns and has conducted extensive educational seminars and cat grooming and behavioral workshops.

The publisher gratefully acknowledges the kind permission granted to reprint the following copyrighted material. Should any copyright holder have been inadvertently omitted, they should apply to the publisher who will be pleased to credit them in full in any subsequent editions.

William Ralph Inge, *Rustic Moralist*: from *A Rustic Moralist* by William Ralph (Dean) Inge. Copyright 1937. Reprinted with permission of G.P. Putnam & Sons.

Fernand Méry, "Her Majesty the Cat" by Fernand Méry. Reprinted with permission of Éditions Robert Laffont.

Carl Van Vechten, "The Exemplary Cat": from *The Tiger in the House* by Carl Van Vechten. Copyright 1920, 1936 by Carl Van Vechten. Reprinted by permission of Alfred A. Knopf, Inc.

9-Lives is a registered trademark of Heinz Pet Products, an affiliate of H.J. Heinz Co.

Fancy Feast is a registered trademark of Friskies Petcare Co.

Louis Weber, C.E.O.
Publications International, Ltd.
7373 North Cicero Avenue
Lincolnwood, Illinois 60646

Manufactured in U.S.A.

8 7 6 5 4 3 2 1

ISBN: 0-7853-1411-3

Contents

INTRODUCTION

From mankind's earliest beginnings, the cat has touched the human soul. The growls and prowls of early felines thrilled our ancestors, who both envied and feared her grace and exquisite prowess. Yet whether revered as a feline god or reviled as the devil's own, the cat has kept her own counsel and endured with a dignified purr. Her legends echo through the halls of time, stirring the passions of one and all and painting our very lives, language, customs, and even our religions with feline color.

Cats traded an uncertain future in the wild for a sheltered, more comfortable existence cuddling in the laps of humankind. And we, in turn, have brought the panther into the parlor. We humans revel in the wild child who purrs her love into our ears at night. It's arguable which one of us got the better deal.

Today, there are over 100 distinct breeds of domestic cats, all but a pawstep away from their wild brethren. The feral cats our ancestors both worshiped and persecuted have evolved into the pampered designer pets who now share our lives. Yet whether longhaired, shorthaired, curlyhaired, bald, with or without tails, solid-colored, striped, or spotted, cats remain the beloved of the enlightened among us—regardless of which stylish look they may sport.

Despite our affection for each other, humans and cats still struggle at times for a proper meeting of the minds. Meows only go so far, and we have yet to unravel all the mysteries of the intricacies of cat-speak.

Feline behaviors are endlessly fascinating and mysterious to humans, who long to understand the exotic speech of whisker twitches, tail quivers, trilling purrs, and paw swipes. Since cats struggle valiantly to understand the strange goings-on of the humans in their care, it seems only just that we strive to decipher the gentle language of the cat.

Even more than this, humans remain in awe of the acute senses that cats possess: eyes that see in the darkest hour, ears that detect the slightest whisper, and a nose that unravels the most delicate trace. Compared to our cats, we humans are blind, deaf, and scent-dumb. We must appear particularly dense to our cats. The cat's keen senses and profound expressions strengthen our belief that kitty has a sixth sense. Whether kitty inherited these extrasensory perceptions from her majestic ancestors or whether some scientific theory exists to explain her special gift, we may never fully comprehend the cat's mystical abilities.

Is it any wonder then that the naming of a cat is serious business? A name must capture that combination of angel and imp found within every cat yet be distinctive unto the individual. In truth, cats are particular about their names. Choose unwisely and kitty may turn deaf ears to it; pick with perception and kitty will visibly puff with pride and eagerly respond to the chosen moniker.

Even as her impish nature gleams from stunning eyes, kitty's generous nature trills a purr able to calm the mightiest human anger or soothe the deepest heartache. That wee beast so often accused of having an aloof, independent nature seems to know when we need a cuddle. That she should choose to spend one of her precious nine lives with us is, indeed, a great gift.

In answer, we humans celebrate our love of all the special cats in our lives. Cats star in our literature, music, and art. The enormous appeal of everything feline is reflected in countless products linked to kitty's charming ways. Even modern entertainment—television, film, and theater—has not escaped the mark of the captivating cat.

No other animal in history has been so exalted or so despised. Today, no longer a devil or a god, the cat has taken her rightful place as a beloved companion. She amuses us with her games, cheers us with her blithe spirit, soothes our anger, and comforts our sorrow. She gives her love freely yet remains faithful to herself. In return, we offer her shelter, care, protection, and unbounded affection. This we give and more, all for the love of cats.

History of the Cat

She had green eyes, that excellent seer,
And little peaks to either ear.
She sat there, and I sat here.
She spoke of Egypt, and a white
Temple, against enormous night.
She smiled with clicking teeth and said
That the dead were never dead;
She said old emperors hung like bats
In barns at night, or ran like rat—
But empresses came back as cat!

Stephen Vincent Benet

ORIGINS: FROM THE DAWN OF TIME

The earliest forebear of the cat sprang from the misty beginnings of time itself. All modern cats are descendants of a tiny, shrewlike creature called a miacid, which first appeared 61 million years ago. These ferocious creatures lived in forests; their retractable claws and agile bodies made them equally at home hunting on the ground or scrambling through the trees. Due to their larger brains, the miacids became expert hunters and outlived other carnivorous mammals.

Forty million years ago, the miacids evolved into a variety of carnivores. Some of these descendants, such as the ancient civet cat, were the first members of the

This fellow looks more like something kitty would catch and eat, doesn't he? In fact the miacid, the great-great-grandaddy of all cats, was probably about the same size as modern mice or shrews. Yet he was the earliest meat eater and founded all modern day carnivores. But rather than chowing down on prehistoric steak, these early carnivores primarily munched insects. Miacids scurried through the underbrush or scrambled up into trees looking for buggy prey. Do you suppose that's why modern day cats still relish an occasional crunchy snack of cricket?

A variety of meat-eating animals evolved from the miacids. From these new creatures sprang all the modern families of the order carnivora, *including this African civet cat. Actually, this intense-looking creature isn't a cat at all. Rather than belonging to the family* felidae *like our cats, this distant cat cousin belongs to the family* viverridae, *which includes the civet, genet, and mongoose. Other land creatures descended from tiny miacids include raccoons, bears, weasels and badgers, hyenas, and even dogs and wolves. Yes, that's right—cats and dogs are kissing cousins! (Well, maybe not.)*

Felidae (cat) family. The *Smilodon,* slow, dim-witted saber-toothed cats, appeared about 34 million years ago. Swift, intelligent *Pseudaelurus* prowled the earth about the same time and survived their saber-toothed cousins. This big cat looked much like modern day cats; it is most likely that all existing felines evolved from this animal.

The machairodontinae *family consisted of cats with large saberlike upper canine teeth that couldn't be used unless they held their mouth wide open. The most advanced of these cats was the* Smilodon. *He employed his huge teeth as stabbing weapons and relied on massive neck muscles to deliver penetrating blows. His prey were the slow-moving mammoths and mastodons. Although saber-toothed cats were ferocious, they died out early. Excavations have revealed that saber-toothed cats often became trapped and died when they followed mammoths into tar pits.*

TRUE CATS: WILD TO DOMESTIC

The oldest recovered fossils of true cats date back 12 million years. Those fossils include members of the three main cat groups: *Acinonyx* (cheetah), *Panthera* (great cats), and *Felis* (small cats). From the *Felis* group came the wild cat which traveled throughout Europe, Asia, and Africa. It is the African wild cat that is the granddaddy of all domestic varieties. This sand-colored tabby domesticated itself about 3,500 years ago, trading a walk on the wild side for "mousy" rewards found in the grain stores of Egypt.

Over time, these domesticated cats reached other countries. They were smuggled out of Egypt, under penalty of death to the smuggler, to India and China. Phoenician traders carried cats on their ships to various parts of the world, and the cats spread slowly across Europe making their way to England. Eventually, the colonists brought cats with them to the New World.

There are more than 25 subspecies of wild cats found in Asia, Europe, Africa, and America. There has long been speculation that one or more of these small wild felines gave rise to the first domesticated cats so treasured in ancient Egypt. The African wild cat (felis silvestris lybica) *is considered the most likely forebear of the first domesticated cats. He is easily tamed, and although a bit bigger than our house cats, he has similar anatomical features. Further evidence supports this theory. Many of the mummified cats found in tombs of ancient Egypt have been identified as African wild cats.*

What sort of philosophers are we, who know absolutely nothing of the origin and destiny of cats?

Henry David Thoreau

Showing ferocious teeth is enough for close range, but the roar of this lioness scares anyone even long distances away. The lion, tiger, jaguar, and leopard are the only cats capable of the earth-rattling roar. The roar is possible because of a series of bones called the hyoid that supports the larynx. A long, elastic ligament that connects the hyoid bones produces the roar. The hyoid bones in small cats, like our house cats, are inflexible and only able to produce a scream. In the lion, the ligament is six inches long but stretches to nine inches to allow a larger air passage for roaring that carries up to five miles.

RELIGION: FROM DEITY TO DEVIL

Ancient mankind honored and revered cats for their extraordinary hunting prowess, but it was the cat's mystical qualities that prompted early Egypt to set it on a pedestal. About 950 B.C., a cat goddess called Bast (or Pasht) was worshiped in the city of Bubastis. Bast was favored by the sun-god Ra and was identified with the life-giving warmth of the sun. She was also associated with good health, music and dancing, happiness, and pleasure and was a symbol of motherhood and fertility.

A temple was built in Bast's honor, and sacred cats were kept in high style in the temple. Each mew, tail swish, and whisker flick was interpreted by the priests as a message sent from the goddess. Cats were held in such reverence that killing a cat carried the death penalty. Deep mourning followed the death of a cat, which was then mummified and entombed.

Cats were often mummified in ancient Egypt, just as their human owners were. The ceremony prepared the cats for life in the next world. Their bodies were treated with preservatives, then wound in sheets of linen. The final outer covering could be cloth, papyrus, or palm leaves; two colors were sometimes woven together to represent a coat pattern. Cloth or palm leaves were attached to form upright ears, and sometimes feline faces were painted on the covering.

This statue represents the cat goddess of ancient Egypt known as Bast. Bast was the representative of the moon, which was considered the sun-god's eye during the hours of the night. It was believed that Bast cradled the sun in her eyes at night. She kept watch with this light given to her and used her great claws to battle the sun's deadly enemy—the serpent of darkness. Each night she vanquished the serpent enemy, allowing the sun to arise reborn each morning.

Early Egyptians weren't alone in their worship of the cat. Birman cats guarded the Buddhist temple of Lao-Tsun, and Siamese were the cherished companions of royalty in ancient Siam. Cats were thought to serve as a bridge between this world and the next. When members of the royal house of Siam were buried, a favorite cat was entombed alive with them. The roof of the tomb contained small holes, and if the cat managed to escape, the priests knew the human soul had passed into the cat's body. These venerated cats were then cared for in the temple. When they finally died, they conducted the human soul into paradise.

Early Christianity at first welcomed the cat as a symbol of motherhood linked to the Madonna. The "good" cat's war upon "bad" mice embodied the church's struggle to overcome evil. But the early Middle Ages saw an end to the cat's truce with Christianity. Threatened by anything linked to pagan religions, the church denounced cats as profane. By the 13th century, cats were linked to devil worship, sorcery, and every evil imaginable. Thousands of cats were tortured and killed in the name of religion.

When a cat died, a wise Egyptian tried to be someplace else so that he couldn't be accused of its murder.

Herodotus

A gold headdress from Colombia, circa. A.D. 400–700, features a feline motif. Wild cats figured prominently in early religions. Jaguars and eagles were the symbols of the two orders of the Aztec warrior knights. During the 6th century B.C., the Chavin people of Peru worshiped a cougar god. The Zapotecs of ancient Mexico honored a jaguar god called Cosijo.

Cats have succeeded one another through the Tertiary epoch for probably millions of years, and in their capacity as butchering machines have undergone a steady improvement.

Thomas Henry Huxley (1825–1895), English Scientist

Unfortunately for man, the elimination of cats allowed the rats to proliferate. As the Black Plague swept through Europe during the 14th century, cats were needed to kill the plague-carrying rodents. This was the beginning of the end of the cat's suffering. The cat's ghastly fall from grace ended by the 17th century when cats again became popular pets.

An Italian mosaic celebrates a cat's great hunting prowess. Even the older paintings on tombs in ancient Egypt illustrate cats who seem to be leaping into the air to knock down birdy prey, then retrieving it for their owners. But for the most part, cats were prized as protectors of grain. Mousers were good, but the cat able to kill rats was even more highly prized. Cats with singed tails were considered less valuable, for it was thought if kitty slept so soundly that close to the fire, he couldn't be too great a hunter.

Cats around the world relish fish, as does this Indian feline. Although the first domestic cats from ancient Egypt were jealously guarded, some were stolen and the species soon spread throughout the world. Cats reached India around 200 B.C. From India, the cat traveled to China and Japan, then Greece, the Mediterranean, and finally Europe. Sailors traveling to the Middle East inadvertently brought back rats on their ships. To combat the rodents, cats were invited along for the ride, and ships' cats were consequently distributed around the world. Eventually, cold climates gave rise to longhaired cats like Persians, while other areas produced tailless kitties and other varieties. History has indeed left its mark on the cat.

A cat is a lion in a jungle of small bushes.

Indian proverb

Design of the Cat

Some pussies' coats are yellow;
Some amber streaked with dark,
No member of the feline race but has a special mark.
This one has feet with hoarfrost tipped;
That one has tail that curls;
Another's inky hide is striped;
Another's decked with pearls.

Anonymous

BODY TYPES

All cats have the same type of skeleton and muscle system; the only differences are in the length and thickness of the bones and the heaviness or elongation of the muscle structure. These minor differences account for the major body differences seen in the various breeds. The short, thick-boned cats with heavy muscles, such as the Manx and Cymric, are at one end of the physical spectrum while the long, fine-boned cats with elongated muscles, such as the Siamese and Orientals, are at the other end.

The shortest bodied cats are called *cobby*. They

This classic longhaired Persian displays the cobby *body type. The stockiest cats are the Manx and Cymric, and the heaviest boned of the cobby cats are the Exotic Shorthair, Himalayan, and Persian. The medium-boned, smaller Burmese is also short-bodied and part of the cobby type.*

are usually heavy-boned and medium to large in size with a round head. Cobby cats usually have a short, thick tail with a rounded end. The exceptions are the Manx and Cymric, which are tailless cats.

Heavy-boned and short-bodied cats that are not extremely cobby fall into a *semicobby* body type. They have a round head and a thick tail that may have a rounded tip like a Bombay's or a tapering tip like a Singapura's.

A Longhaired Scottish Fold has the characteristic sturdy, round body described as semicobby. *The American Bobtail, American Shorthair, American Wirehair, Bombay, Chartreux, British Shorthair, Scottish Fold, and the very short-legged Munchkin are the other breeds that fall into this category. Smaller semicobby cats include the Korat and Singapura.*

Large and sturdy cats are long-bodied and heavy-boned with a broad chest and rib cage. Although they have an elongated body, they usually are not slender or small. The exception is the Ocicat, which is narrow across the back, rib cage, and chest.

The Maine Coon is an example of a large and sturdy *cat. This elongated body type is generally muscular. As the cat's body becomes longer, the tail usually follows suit. Other large and sturdy breeds include the Norwegian Forest Cat, Ocicat, Ragdoll, and the somewhat smaller Birman.*

As a cat's body elongates, the boning tends to become more elongated also. Cats in this category are called *semiforeign*. These cats are medium- to fine-boned with an angular or rounded head and a slender or thick tail.

Cats with the *foreign* body type have a longer, slender body, fine bones, and a wedge-shaped angular head. They may also have some rounded features such as the rounded cheekbones and rounded rump of the Japanese Bobtail.

The most slender, fine-boned, and angular cats were formerly called foreign. Due to breeding practices and the refining of foreign features, they are now in a class of their own called *Oriental*. These cats are small, long, and sleek with a long wedge-shaped head, a thin tapering tail, and small oval feet.

This fine-boned yet muscular Russian Blue displays the foreign *body type. Cats in this category have a long, slim build. The Abyssinian, Cornish Rex, Japanese Bobtail, Longhaired Russian Blue, Somali, and Turkish Angora are included in this group.*

Above: *The Tonkinese has a* semiforeign *body, which is halfway between the Oriental body of the Siamese and the cobby body of the Burmese. Also of a semiforeign body type are the American Curl, Bengal, California Spangle, Devon Rex, Havana, Snowshoe, Sphynx, and Turkish Van.*

Opposite page: *Cats that have a lithe, slim body, slanted eyes, large, pointed ears, and fine, short fur, such as this Siamese, are of the* Oriental *body type. Other cats in this category are the Balinese, Oriental Shorthair, and Oriental Longhair.*

COAT TYPES, COLORS & PATTERNS

The first thing you notice about a cat is her distinctive fur coat; it's her pride and joy. But kitty's magnificent coat isn't just for good looks, it also protects her from heat and cold. Over the years, environmental adaptation and selective breeding have created a wide array of coat types, colors, and patterns.

When a cat has all the same colored hairs from the root to the tip, the coat color and pattern is called *solid*. Solid colors are black, blue, chocolate, lilac, red, cream, and white. True solid red, cream, chocolate, and lilac are impossible to achieve since these colors always show some variation.

A gradual variation in the color of a cat's coat is called shading. There are three different *shaded* patterns. *Chinchilla* shading appears as sparkling white with a hint of color. *Shaded* cats seem to have a veil of color over them. *Smoke* cats

This Siamese features a pointed color pattern in solid blue. Her light coat shows the excellent contrast with the blue points on her face, ears, feet, and tail. Although it may not be immediately apparent, Burmese cats also display a pointed color pattern. They have sepia points, *which means the point color on their face, ears, feet, and tail is a darker version of their body color. Because of this, sepia point cats may appear to be solid-colored. Tonkinese cats sometimes feature a* mink point *pattern, which is a cross between the sepia and pointed colors.*

appear to be solid-colored until you "blow" back the coat and the underneath is white.

Tortoiseshell cats have a coat with a combination of any one solid color and red or cream. These colors may be completely mixed as in brindled tortoiseshell or separate as in patched tortoiseshell. The solid color may be black, brown, blue, chocolate, lilac, cinnamon, fawn, or golden.

Tabby cats come in all colors and patterns. The *classic tabby* pattern features a combination of stripes and circles. The *mackerel tabby* pattern has more clearly defined stripes than the classic tabby. The *spotted tabby* pattern has spots in various sizes and shapes. A *patched tabby,* also called a *torbie,* is a mixture of tabby markings on tortoiseshell colors and patterns.

Any cat's coat that has some white on it is called a *parti-color.* The most common pattern in parti-colors is the *bicolor,* which is two-thirds color or pattern and one-third white or just the opposite. The second most recognized pattern is *van,* which is all white with the color or pattern appearing only on the top of the head and along the length of the tail. The third pattern is called

Cats come in a variety of coat types—from longhair to shorthair and anything in between. This Maine Coon wears a long, shaggy coat. The American Wirehair is the only cat with a midlength, wirehaired coat. Rexed coats come in tightly curled, soft waves as on the Cornish Rex and plush, downy waves as on the Devon Rex. Some kitties have no fur at all. The Sphynx cat is a hairless cat with only a light layering of downlike hairs on some portions of the body.

harlequin. It consists of an all white coat with small patches of alternating colors or patterns starting on the top of the head and alternating down the body to the tip of the tail.

Pointed colors are those colors or patterns restricted to the ears, face, legs, feet, and tail of a cat with the body being a corresponding yet much lighter shade. There are several types of pointed colors. *Solid* points come in colors of seal, blue, chocolate, lilac, red, cream, and cinnamon. *Lynx* points come in tabby colors. *Tortie* points appear as tortoiseshell colors. *Sepia* points are not easily seen since they are only slightly darker than the body color. Sepia points come in sable, blue, champagne (or chocolate), platinum, red, cream, cinnamon, and tortoiseshell colors. *Mink* points are created by combining sepia and pointed colors. Mink point colors are called mink or natural mink, blue mink, champagne or chocolate mink, honey mink, and platinum mink.

This Abyssinian features a ticked *or* agouti *pattern, meaning that individual hairs are striped with bands of different colors. Tipping occurs when hairs have one band of color. There are three degrees of tipping.* Chinchilla *has color just on the very ends,* shaded *has color from the tip to about midway down the hair shaft, and* smoke *has color from the tip to three-quarters down the hair shaft.*

Solid Black

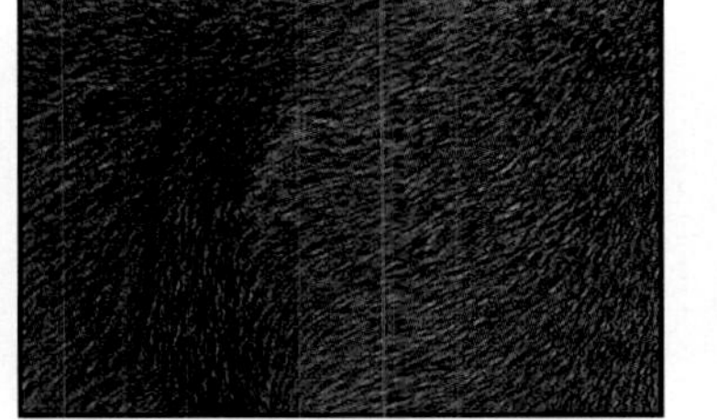
Solid Blue

Solid Lilac

Solid Cream

Shaded

Chinchilla

Smoke

Tortoiseshell

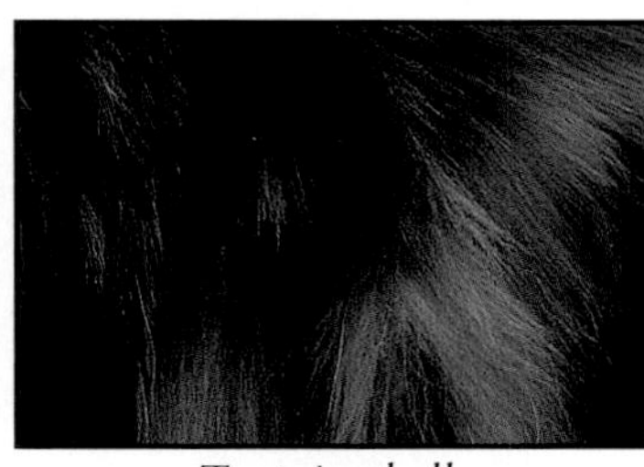
Tortoiseshell

Blue Tortie

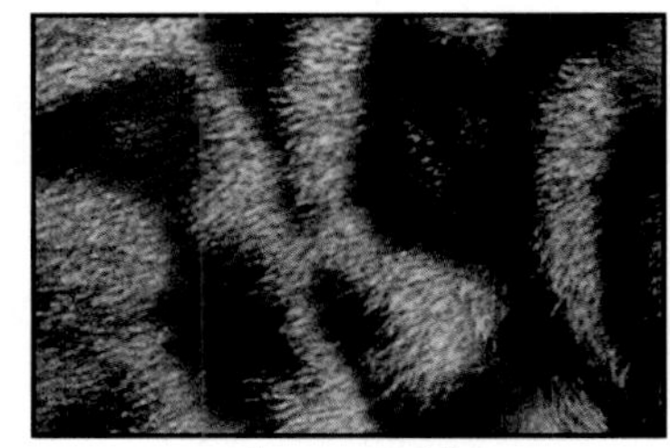
Classic Tabby

Classic Tabby

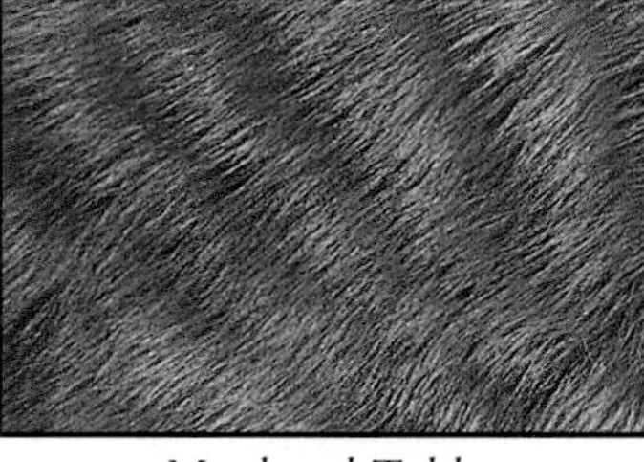
Mackerel Tabby

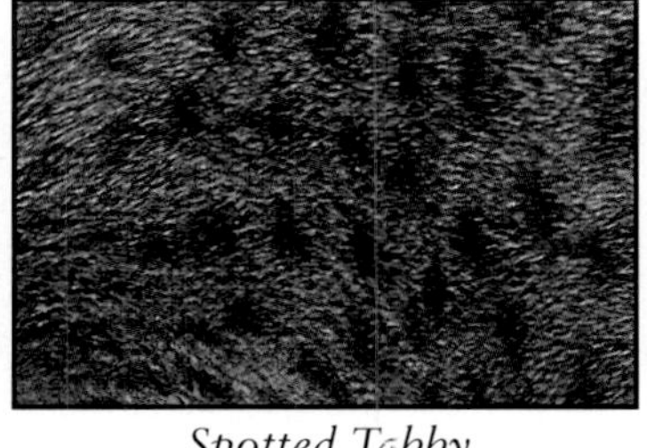
Spotted Tabby

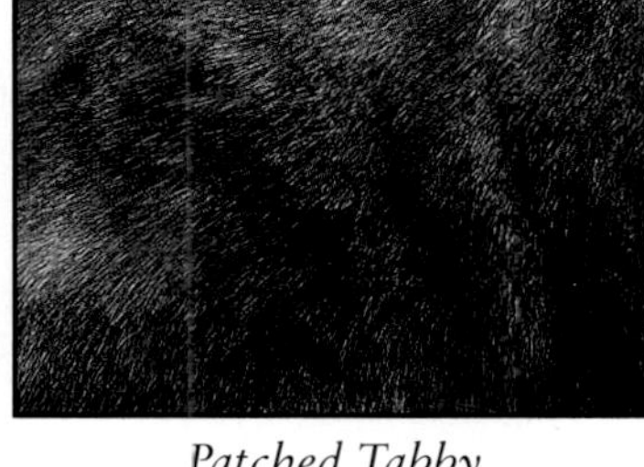
Patched Tabby

Bicolor

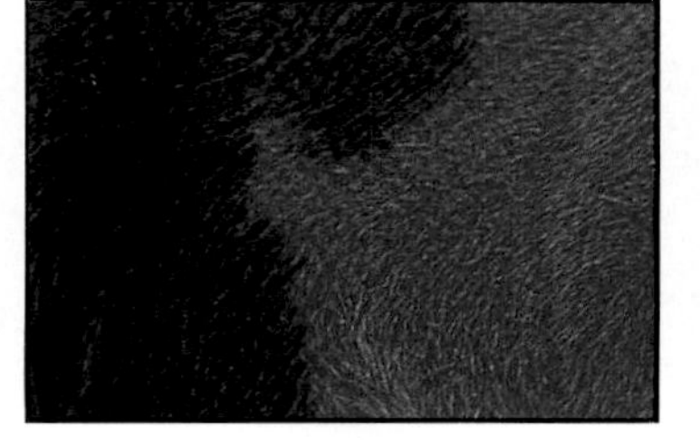
Bicolor

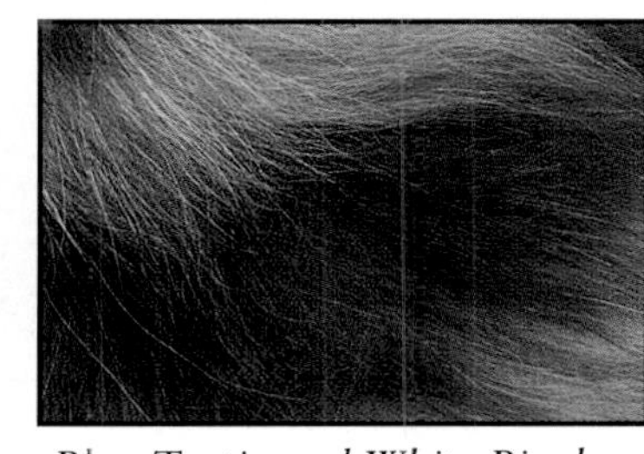
Blue Tortie and White Bicolor

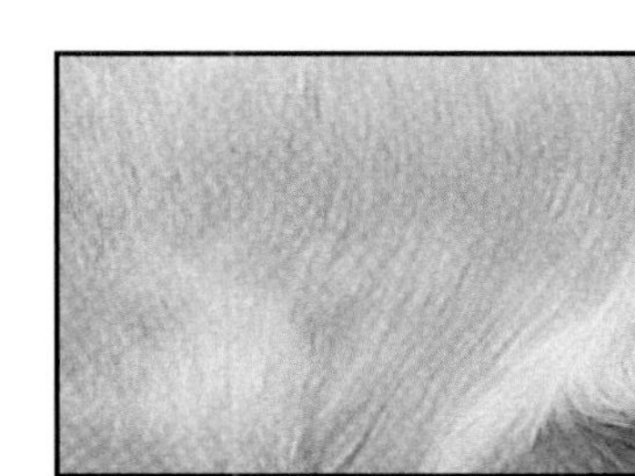
Van

Harlequin

EYE COLORS & SHAPES

The color of a cat's eyes is determined genetically and varies by breed. The pigment cells in the iris produce the cat's eye color. The magnificent range of cats' eye colors depends on the amount of pigment, the position of the pigment, and the distribution of the light reflected from the pigment. Albino cats have pinkish-red eyes due to lack of pigment. Blue eyes are due not only to the light dispersion but also to the color density at the back of the eye.

Cats' eyes may be large, medium, or small, but all cats have round eyes. What makes them appear to be different shapes are the eye openings, the upper and lower eyelids, and the position of the eyes. There are three basic eye shapes: round, oval, and almond. Some eyes are positioned very far apart and others are close together—the closest being only one eye width apart as in the Balinese.

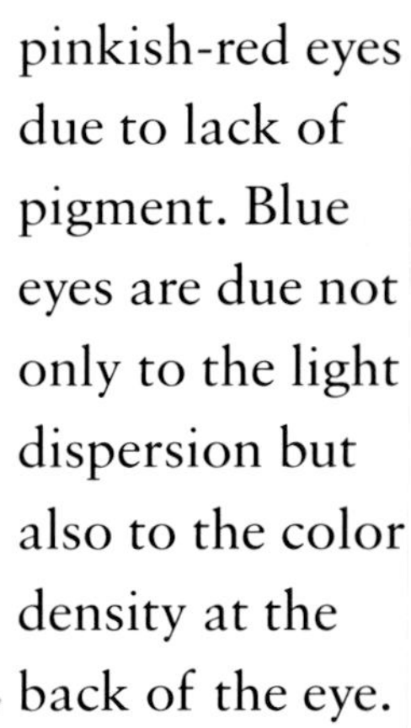

This American Shorthair displays the flattened oval-shaped eyes typical of this breed. Cats have three basic eye shapes with variations of each shape. Korats have large, round eyes while Ragdolls have oval-shaped eyes. Orientals appear to have almond-shaped eyes since the eyes are slanted and set to the side of the head. Just as there are different eye shapes, there are many distinct eye colors. Cats' eyes can range in color—anything from copper to blue. The chart on the opposite page shows just some of the many possible variations.

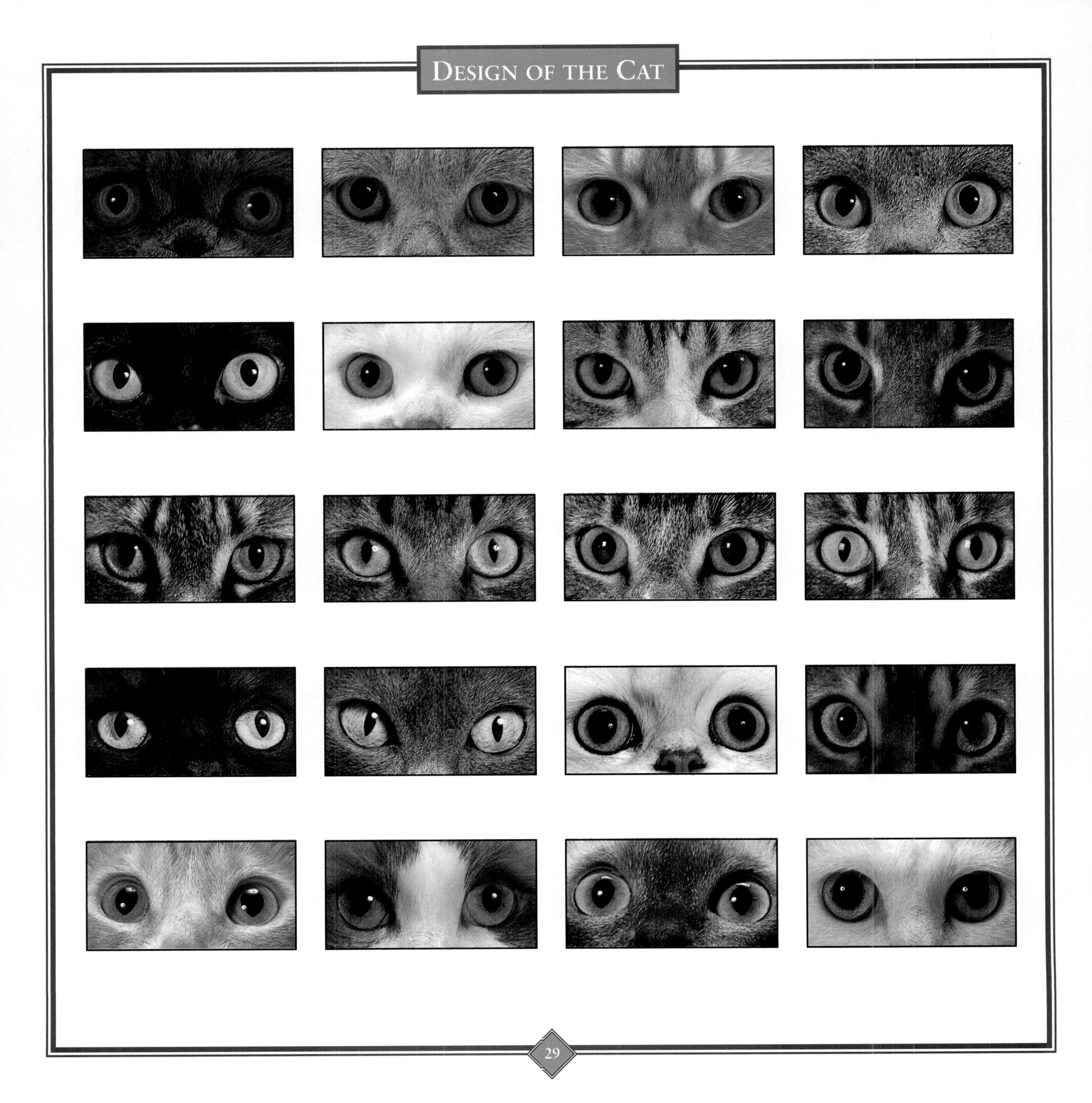

Breeds

Once it has given its love,
what absolute confidence,
what fidelity of affection!
It will make itself the companion
of your hours of work, of loneliness, or of sadness.
It will lie the whole evening on your knee,
purring and happy in your society,
and leaving the company of creatures
of its own society to be with you.

Théophile Gautier

The Munchkin is a new short-legged breed. Sometimes called the Dachshund Cat or a Robust Basset, this breed is a genetic mutation of a gene similar to the one that produces Corgi, Basset, and Dachshund dogs. Munchkins appeared in Great Britain during the 1930s and 1940s but died out during the war. They reappeared in Russia in 1953, but nothing was done to perpetuate them. They appeared again in 1991 in the United States, and they are now registerable in several associations. The Ojos Azules is another new breed and has striking blue eyes and a white-tipped tail. The recently developed Pixie Bob comes in three hair lengths: shorthair, middlehair, and longhair.

Europe, the Burmilla (a chinchilla silver short-haired cat) has been produced and is gaining popularity. In North America, many new breeds are seeking to become recognized for showing. They include the Honey Bear (a Persian-style cat), the La Perm (a longhair Rex), and the Ural Rex (a shorthair Rex).

ABYSSINIAN

One of the oldest recognized breeds is the Abyssinian. In 1860, a cat called Zula was brought from Abyssinia to Great Britain. This cat had a unique ticked coat and was bred with other cats with similar markings. From these matings, the Abyssinian breed was produced.

This breed has a warm brown coat that has several bands of color on each hair. The Abyssinian's ticked pattern and muscular body give it the appearance of a small cougar cat.

Abys are one-person cats and will pick their favorite human out of a family. They are alert, intelligent, and sensitive to their person's moods. They will tolerate other cats but are not group oriented. They are quiet-voiced yet have an extremely active nature. These cats do not like to cuddle; but they will march up your lap, put their paws on your chest, and demand to be petted while purring up a storm.

This regal ruddy Abyssinian poses in a posture similar to the ancient Egyptian statues of the cat goddess, Bast. Maybe kitty is remembering her royal days back in the land of the Nile. Some believe the Abyssinian cat was the Bast cat worshiped in ancient Egypt. This could be because Abyssinians resemble the Egyptian Kephyr cats in color and body type. The ancient Egyptians used Kephyr cats as eliminators of disease-carrying pests. These cats were considered gods, and to harm or steal one resulted in a death sentence. Majestic as this Aby may seem, behind her glowing eyes and mischievous grin is a fun-loving, very active personality.

As kittens, Abyssinians are frequently referred to as chipmunks. This "chipmunk" is a ruddy Abyssinian kitten who already displays the ticked coat, dark tail tip, and toe webbings called for in showcats. Abyssinians have a moderately foreign body type. They are very lithe and limber but are not as elongated as an Oriental. Their coat is short yet rich and full with a reddish undercoat called ruddy. They come in ruddy, blue, red, and tortoiseshell. Active and frisky as kittens, these cats retain their love for play as they mature. Of all the breeds, Abys are the most demonstrative of their love for their person.

AMERICAN BOBTAIL

The large and sturdy American Bobtail first appeared in Arizona around the 1960s. Tailless cats were unique enough to stand out as different; since this cat did not resemble an existing breed, American cat fanciers began the difficult and time-consuming task of genetically "setting" this cat to meet show standards. The first cat of this breed was named Yodie, and he is considered the original "father" to the first American Bobtails. Now in the 1990s, this new breed is striving for worldwide acceptance.

Although American Bobtails are independent cats, they do enjoy the company of others and are easily trained. Despite their size, they are affectionate and gentle, and they like to curl up next to their person for love—and cozy naps.

American Bobtails come in all colors and patterns; this longhaired Bobtail sports a seal lynx point coat. Besides the variety of coat colors, this breed's most recognizable feature is its short, bobbed tail. As with other breeds that have a unique characteristic, there's an imaginative cat "tail" that explains the origin of this bobtailed cat. The original cat of this breed was guarding a farmer's sleeping baby, and a bear in a bad mood came along. When the cat defended the child, the ruckus brought the farmer running with his shotgun to drive the bear off. Instead, it was the cat who lost two-thirds of his tail.

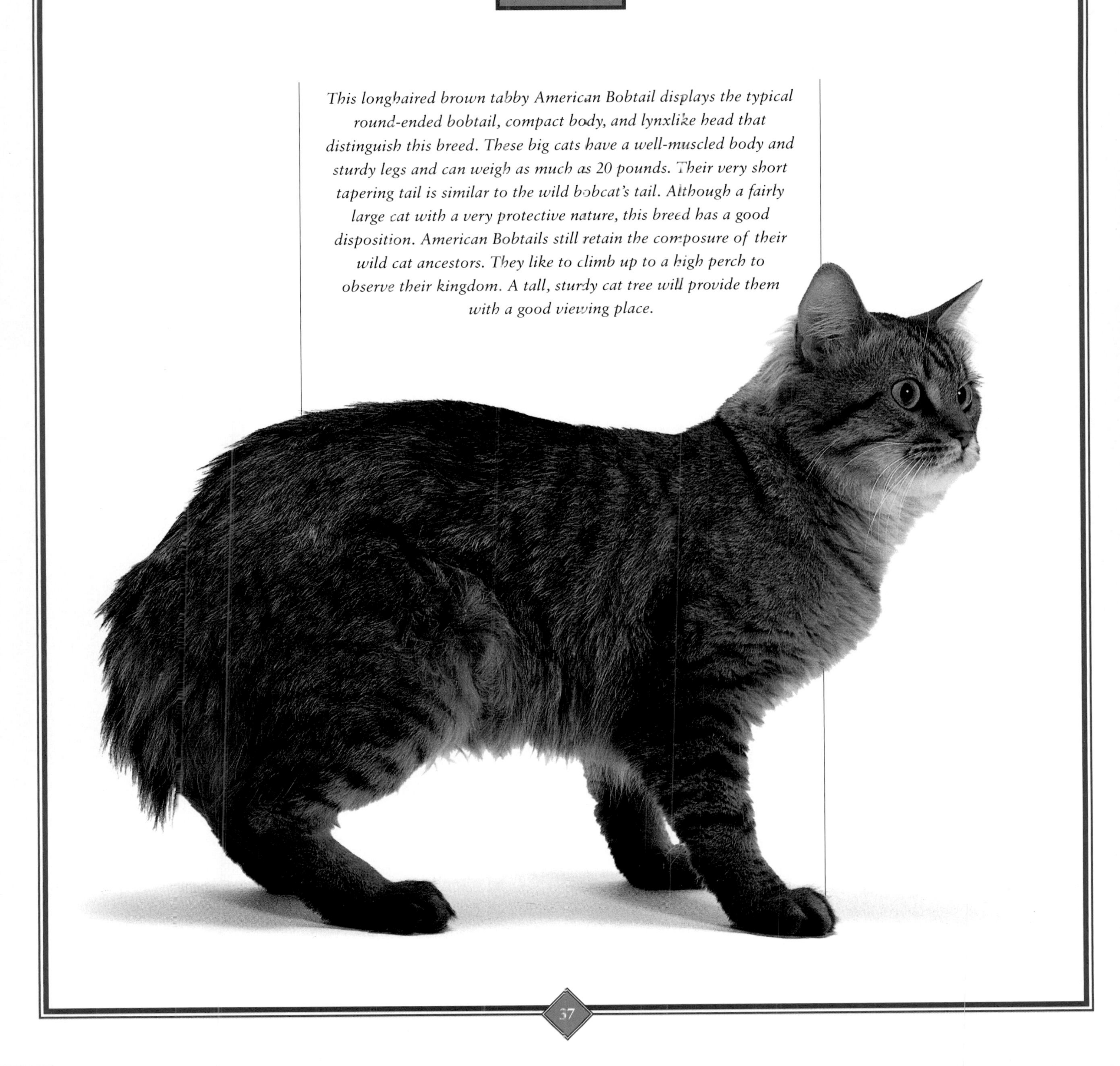

This longhaired brown tabby American Bobtail displays the typical round-ended bobtail, compact body, and lynxlike head that distinguish this breed. These big cats have a well-muscled body and sturdy legs and can weigh as much as 20 pounds. Their very short tapering tail is similar to the wild bobcat's tail. Although a fairly large cat with a very protective nature, this breed has a good disposition. American Bobtails still retain the composure of their wild cat ancestors. They like to climb up to a high perch to observe their kingdom. A tall, sturdy cat tree will provide them with a good viewing place.

AMERICAN CURL

Another newcomer to the show bench is the American Curl. This breed started with a genetic mutation found on a domestic cat. In 1981, a female longhair stray with curled-back ears was adopted by a family who named her Shulamith. Cat fanciers began the necessary breeding programs in an attempt to isolate this new ear type. Both longhair and shorthair varieties were produced and eventually accepted for championship exhibition in the late 1980s.

American Curls are outgoing "people" cats. They are healthy cats with a sunny disposition. They love to sit on their person's lap and shoulders. They enjoy the company of young children and other cats. American Curls are fairly active and maintain their playful activities throughout their adult life. They are easily trained and make good travelers.

The shorthaired American Curl has short ear tufts that form an aureole of hair around the ears, and this brown tabby displays them to good advantage. This kitty's sweet expression is typical of the lovable disposition of this recently recognized breed. The American Curl's unique ears are upright and the outer edge curls backward, away from the head. The ears start to curl at four to seven days of age. This unusual curling is caused by a genetic mutation and does not affect the cat's hearing or the mobility of the ears. Some say that since the cats originated on the windy seaside cliffs of California, their ears were blown backward by the strong ocean gales and then stayed that way.

A longhaired seal point American Curl strikes an appealing pose that shows off the lovely backward curl of the ears. American Curls have a slender, lithe body and an angular (modified wedge) head. They have either a short, rich resilient coat with a long tail or a long, silky coat with very long, full tail hair like this kitty. These sweet cats come in all colors and patterns, and their expressive eyes range from gold to blue.

This attractive torbie spotted American Curl displays the curled ears, muttonchop whiskers, ear tufts, and brush tail typical of the longhaired variety of this breed. Kitty has jumped up on his hind legs as if to say, "I need love and attention." These well-muscled cats are personable, gentle, and fun-loving. They are very curious and quite playful. American Curls are excellent companions. Normal petting is all the grooming they require to keep their coats polished, but trimming their toenails about once every three weeks is recommended.

AMERICAN SHORTHAIR

When the Mayflower reached the shores of the New World, the ancestor of the American Shorthair stepped onto Plymouth Rock with the rest of the pilgrims. This hardy cat started out as a mouser, keeping farms and homes free from vermin. The first registered American Shorthair came from a pedigreed bloodline introduced from England in 1900. Called a Domestic Shorthair until the early 1970s, the breed began to gain devotees and was the first shorthaired cat listed by the newly formed Cat Fanciers Association in 1904.

American Shorthairs are affectionate, head-butting cats that love to be petted. They have an easygoing temperament and are intelligent and friendly. They have retained their keen hunting abilities and are athletic cats. They have a low, well-modulated voice but are not talkers. They enjoy other cats and thrive in their company.

This silver tabby American Shorthair displays the strong body, orange-shaped head, and shiny coat that is characteristic of this breed. The classic tabby pattern combined with the silver coloring has become the most popular design for this breed. As kittens, American Shorthairs are tiny; they slowly develop to their robust adult size. They are much more playful and active as kittens than as mature cats. These hardy cats are affectionate and very loyal, yet they are independent and tend to rule their households with an "iron paw." They are loving to their family but suspicious of strangers until they have been properly introduced.

AMERICAN WIREHAIR

The first truly new American cat breed is the American Wirehair. This breed was a spontaneous mutation that appeared in a litter of wirehaired kittens born to a pair of straight-haired farm cats in New York. A wire-coated male kitten from the litter, Council Rock Farm Adam of Hi-Fi, was used to develop the breed; in 1966, Adam made his appearance to herald the start of a new breed. Although American Wirehairs were granted championship status in 1977, they are still considered a fairly rare breed.

American Wirehairs are independent and will "king" in any group of cats. They are affectionate and loving, but they like to be patted rather than stroked. They are not overly active, and they have a quiet voice. They often take a great interest in their surroundings. American Wirehairs like to play with "teaser" type toys with their person.

With her gold eyes peering intently, this black smoke American Wirehair surveys her kingdom and prepares to do a little exploration. The wiry coat gives the entire body a soft, irregular outline and sets this breed apart from the longhairs, shorthairs, and curly-coated Rexes. The kinking and hooking of the hair is what makes the cat's coat appear extremely short and wiry—similar to a Wirehair Terrier dog's coat. American Wirehairs are affectionately called Wires, and their coat is referred to as a soft "brillo-pad." They do not have to be groomed and are "self-cleaning."

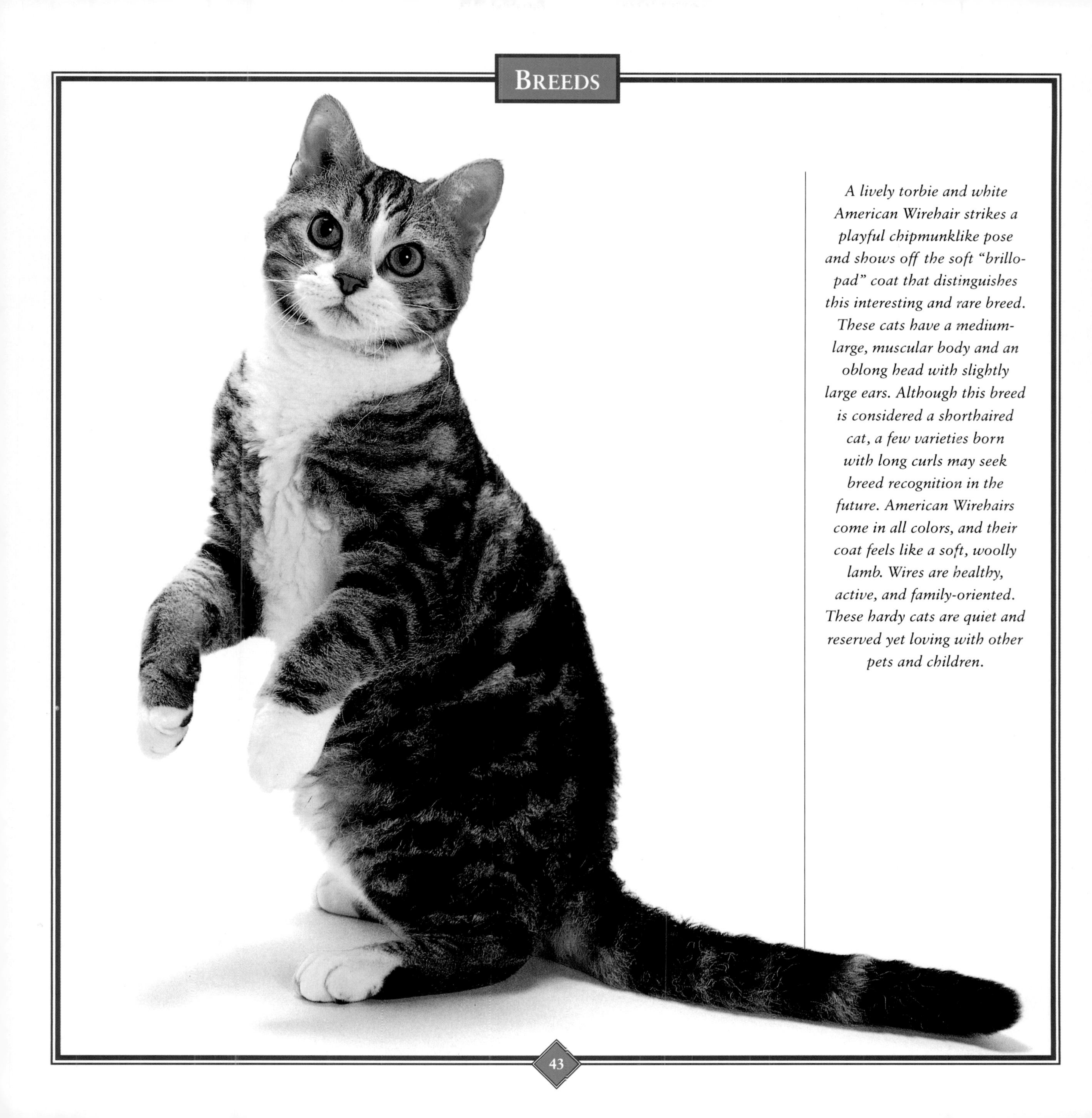

A lively torbie and white American Wirehair strikes a playful chipmunklike pose and shows off the soft "brillo-pad" coat that distinguishes this interesting and rare breed. These cats have a medium-large, muscular body and an oblong head with slightly large ears. Although this breed is considered a shorthaired cat, a few varieties born with long curls may seek breed recognition in the future. American Wirehairs come in all colors, and their coat feels like a soft, woolly lamb. Wires are healthy, active, and family-oriented. These hardy cats are quiet and reserved yet loving with other pets and children.

BALINESE

Balinese cats originated in North America prior to the 1940s, but it wasn't until then that fanciers decided to seriously strive for recognition of this lovely cat. Since certain Siamese bloodlines produced longhaired kittens, it was decided to breed these longhairs to determine if they would breed true; they did and the Balinese was born. Although they are American, they were named after the graceful movement of dancers from the Isle of Bali and the parent Siamese cat. They are now accepted around the world and are a great show favorite.

These cats are talkers and alternate between being extremely active

Resting yet regal, these Balinese are keenly aware of their surroundings. The lilac point cat on the left shows a beautiful wedge-shaped head and soft coat, and the dark seal point cat on the right displays lovely almond-shaped blue eyes. The Balinese is a longhaired version of the Siamese cat and is just as lithe, active, and vociferous. As with the Siamese, these cats love their families and have been known to risk their lives to protect them. Balinese cats are intelligent; they can open doors and drawers with ease, but once they are trained, they remember the words "no" and "come here."

and sedentary. They are curious and extremely intelligent. Balinese cats are also demanding, but they are so lovable and affectionate that their owners will forgive them for anything. They adore their people and are very protective of their human friends. They have even been known to fight off armed burglars.

This lilac point Balinese demonstrates the good contrast between coat color and point colors on her head, tail, and paws. This majestic cat displays all the beauty and elegance that makes this breed popular. Balinese are soft and lovely to look at since the longer hair forms an aureole of softness around their limber form. According to legend, the aureole was referred to as a veil, and the cat's limber body was said to move like that of a Balinese dancer surrounded by her swirling, silken veils. Today it's easy to see that every move these cats make is dancelike—they are truly grace in motion.

From the late 1960s through the 1970s, some cat fanciers desired to create a breed of show-cat with the brilliant coloring and spotting of the leopard. Using small cats such as the Asian leopard cat, experimental matings were attempted by crosses with the American Shorthair, Burmese, Siamese, and others. Most of these breedings resulted in sterile offspring with mackeral tabby stripes, and these bloodlines died out. In 1980, breeders decided to try these experimental matings again using spotted tabby American Shorthairs. Eventually, enough matings produced fertile offspring so that the foundation of the Bengal was assured; no more breed-

The brown spotted, or rosette, pattern on this young cat takes time to develop and will become more prominent as he matures. The beautiful spotted coats of the wild cats have always attracted peoples' eye. In the late '60s and throughout the '70s, various breeds were crossed with the leopard cat, (felis bengalensis) *to produce domesticated cats displaying this type of coat. Thus, the Bengal cat was born. These cats have a striking coat and a long, narrow yet muscular body. They are shorthaired with thick, silky fur and they come in several colors. Bengals resemble miniature jungle cats, and they have become popular show cats.*

ings back to the wild parent were necessary.

While these cats are mischievous and playful, they are not wild and hyperactive. They are curious, gregarious, and affectionate. They love people, dogs, other cats, and children and enjoy playful roughhousing. They demand attention and will climb your leg, begging to be picked up and held.

Two curious Bengal kittens display the differences that can occur in color and pattern between litter mates. The inquisitive cat on the left features a brown marbled pattern, while the youngster on the right presents a cinnamon spotted design. Bengals come in a beautiful spotted pattern or a flowing line pattern called marble. They may display colors such as black on orange (leopard) or brown on cinnamon (sorrel), both with brilliant gold eyes. Sometimes Bengals feature varying dark colors on an ivory background. This coloring is called a snow leopard or snow marble pattern, and cats with this striking design have blue eyes.

BIRMAN

Originally called the Sacred Cat of Burma, the Birman is native to that country and was raised as a temple cat for hundreds of years. The beginning of the Birman line in Europe started with the arrival of a pair of these cats in France in 1919. In 1925, the breed was accepted for showing in France, but it wasn't until 1967 that they were recognized in the United States. During World War II, only one pair of these cats remained in France, and they are the ancestors of all modern Birman cats.

These cats are precocious and even-tempered. They are sweet, loving, and gentle with a quiet intelligence that makes them easily trained. They love people and tolerate other animals. Birman cats have a small voice and a swaggering, tigerlike gait that lends to their regal bearing.

Above: *This beautiful seal point Birman typifies the graceful dignity and silky coat that this breed is known for. Shy with strangers yet devoted to their family, these quiet cats are loving companions to their people and their cat family.*

Opposite page: *The golden body color of the Birman is most apparent on the seal point kitten on the right. Legend explains how this breed received its golden coat. One of the temple cats in ancient Burma, Sinh, was the companion of an elderly priest called Mun-Ha. When raiders attacked the temple, they killed Mun-Ha. Sinh leaped to protect his master. The cat's white coat became golden like the priest's beard, the legs turned brown, and the paws stayed white.*

A black American Shorthair was mated to a sable Burmese in 1958. The resulting kittens became the foundation for the Bombay, which was accepted for championship exhibition in 1969. This breed got its name from the city of Bombay, India, because of its resemblance to the Indian black leopard.

In fact, Bombays are often referred to as small black panthers due to their shiny black coat and brilliant copper eyes. By the 1980s, most registering organizations around the world acknowledged this man-made breed for showing.

These cats are very sweet, smart, and affectionate. They are lap sitters and like to be with other cats. They are excellent with children and make loving pets. Although Bombays are quite strong, they do not like rough play; they are gentle and serene cats.

A top show quality Bombay poses like a panther with his powerful muscles rippling through his gleaming black coat. These sturdy cats have a long, contoured yet stocky body and a round head with wide-set ears. Their almost round eyes range in colors from vivid gold to brilliant copper. Bombays are usually solidly built, and they feel heavier than they look. This breed is recognized for its short, glossy fur, which lies very close to the body. Their thick black coat requires little or no grooming. Despite their powerful looks, Bombays have a docile and affectionate nature, and they crave human companionship.

This Bombay kitten displays the developing musculature, glowing copper eyes, and shiny black coat typical of this breed. The Bombay has been called the "patent leather cat with the copper penny eyes." Although there are no legends concerning this breed as of yet, Bombays' owners seem to feel that these cats bring good luck—and even money—to their home. It has been said that these beautiful cats attract copper pennies. Whether this is true or not, Bombays do bring plenty of love to their household. They are great family companions. They are very playful, but they also enjoy a good cuddle and a warm lap.

BRITISH SHORTHAIR

The British Shorthair is a natural breed that originated in Great Britain. This hardy breed appeared on show benches in the solid black color as early as 1800. By 1889, other colors had been added. North American registering bodies did not accept the British Shorthair for showing until the 1950s. At that time, the British Blue was the only recognized color. By the 1980s, other colors and patterns were allowed to be shown in all North American registries.

British Shorthairs are independent yet very affectionate and loyal. They are people cats first and sometimes like to be group cats. British Shorthairs are gentle, quiet-voiced cats. They love to sit on a windowsill on a sunny day, and they will spend hours admiring the view. If they have an enclosed yard, they will sit outdoors in the sun and survey their kingdom.

This sweet blue and white bicolor British Shorthair kitten is already developing the massive head, round cheeks, short body, and strong legs of this breed. The copper eyes are still baby brown and will turn to a deep copper when this youngster has matured. While British Shorthairs are playful as kittens, they become more sedate and dignified with age. These cats are hardy and strong and make good companions for families with children. They are easy to care for. An occasional brushing is all the care they need—and of course, good food, water, and love.

British Shorthairs are considered Great Britain's national cat, and this lovely tortoiseshell and white kitty makes a great representative for her country. Her round copper eyes reflect good health, intelligence, and the proper coloration for this variety. Brits, as they are affectionately called, have round heads with round-tipped ears and a softly defined muzzle. They have a strong-boned body, sturdy legs, and a medium-short, thick tail like this precious cat. Their full checks, straight nose, and round, alert eyes give them a lively appearance, while their short, plush coat softens their body contours and makes them appear cuddly and warm.

BURMESE

Although the ancestor of the Burmese, a female named Wong Mau, did come from Burma in 1930, this breed owes its development to the American cat fanciers. Wong Mau was crossed with a Siamese sire, and the darkest offspring was retained for further breeding. Eventually, a lovely sable cat was recognized as worthy of exhibition. Between 1947 and 1954, Burmese were exported to other countries, and this popular breed can now be seen worldwide.

Burmese are called Burms in the United States by their owners. They have earned the nickname of the Postage Stamp Cat because they are so affectionate and have to be peeled off their owners. Although they prefer a one-cat home, they integrate well with other cats and animals. These sweet cats are fun-loving and will play a game of fetch with their person.

Above: *The thick sable coat of this young Burmese cat shines like satin. Because of its deep brown color, a Burmese is said to look like a chocolate Easter bunny with short ears and a long tail. This breed has a muscular cobby body and rounded features.*

Opposite page: *This lovable champagne Burmese seems to enjoy the outdoors. Perhaps he has joined his owner for a walk around the yard to check out the garden. The brown colored Burmese was one of the ancient cats that was considered a good luck charm. The sable cats with gold eyes were believed to bring money to their owner.*

CALIFORNIA SPANGLE

One of the most recently developed breeds is the shorthaired California Spangle. These wild-looking cats have a long body, an angular head, and round eyes. Their beautiful spotted coat comes in a variety of colors. The California Spangle has the dubious honor of being the first commercially created cat offered for sale in the Neiman Marcus catalog during the late 1970s. Since good records had been kept of the breed's ancestors, cat fanciers were able to submit the necessary three to five generation pedigrees for show registration. This breed was accepted for championship exhibition in the 1980s.

California Spangles are dominant cats and like to be king of their household. They tolerate other cats and animals but prefer to be the center of attention. They like to be stroked and petted. They are playful and enjoy swinging around on and off their cat tree.

This bronze California Spangle kitten already displays the short forelegs and the emerging spangled pattern of this striking breed. Eventually, kitty's brown eyes will turn into more of a copper color as she matures, and the soft babyish look will be replaced by more wild-looking features. Sometimes called the Spotted Hunter Cat or the Man-Made Leopard, Spangles have a unique feral appearance. They are medium to large in size with an angular head and a long tail. Their lovely coat is short and somewhat dense, and the predominant pattern is dark spots on a lighter background.

A young California Spangle sports a rosette pattern similar to that of wild cats. The California Spangle is a man-made breed created to resemble leopards. Eight different types of domestic cats contributed their characteristics to this new breed. The low carriage and powerful, heavy body of the Spangle cat resembles a feral cat's posture and body. Despite similarities to the great cats, no wild felines were used in the breeding of California Spangles. These cats appear larger and more ferocious than they actually are; in fact, they are quite friendly and affectionate.

CHARTREUX

Chartreux cats are considered an ancient French breed. They were developed in Chartreux, France, by the Carthusian monks. First documented in 1558, the Chartreux is a distinct variety and originally bore its own Latin name, *Felis Catus Cartusianorium*. Although this breed is frequently exhibited as a British or European Shorthair by some registering bodies, it is registered and exhibited as a separate breed by others. In North America, this breed is shown only as a Chartreux.

These cats have a robust nature and are generally quiet, using their expressive eyes and smiling face to get their way. They do well in groups or as lone cats and prefer one person to be their own. They are usually sedentary but like to prowl around their kingdom and check things out.

The Chartreux, the native cat of France, was the first recognized breed in Europe. And this trio of gorgeous Chartreux cats is proud of that fact. They have the plush coat, solid body, and slender legs of their dignified ancestors. The shape of this breed's head and ears blends gently into the soft lines of the body to resemble a monk's hood and robe. The ancient order of the Carthusian monks raised them in the monastery for centuries, and they are still raised there. These cats have been referred to as holy cats because the monks believed the cats kept the monastery holy by keeping vermin out.

CORNISH REX

The first known Cornish Rex was born on a farm in Cornwall, England, in 1950. He was named Kallibunker, and when he was mated back to his mother, more curly-coated kittens were born. This was the start of the first curly-coated cats; up to this time, cats were either long-haired or short-haired. As soon as enough test matings were completed, this rare breed was recognized around the world.

These cats are active, very intelligent, and persistent. They are affectionate and love to play with other cats and people. Although they love children, their small size and delicate bone structure will not withstand rough handling. They are shoulder sitters and great climbers. They love to be on top of objects such as doors, cupboards, and even their person's head. Rex breeds are easy to care for since they shed less than other cats.

With a twitch of her long tail, this lovely black and white Cornish Rex signals that she is about to take off on a mission of exploration. This curious kitty's large ears are pricked to catch every sound. If she stops long enough for you to pet her, you'll notice that kitty's curly fur feels almost like the soft, warm skin of a baby. The lovely curls of the Cornish Rex form gentle waves down the body similar to the curls of the marcel-waved hairstyles worn by the flapper girls of the 1920s.

A tortoiseshell and white Cornish Rex looks at you innocently as if to say, "Who me? Why I'd never get into anything." But those dainty paws can get into a lot. These inquisitive cats love to check everything out. They can use their long "fingers" and their strong chest muscles to pull open just about anything. They have even been rumored to pick a lock with their long, thin manipulative tails. The way those tails seem to kink and curl, that story is almost believable. Playful and affectionate, these delicate cats keep their family amused and entertained.

CYMRIC

Records of the longhaired Manx as well as the traditional shorthaired Manx were listed in the American Cat Association's registry as early as the 1900s. Although the register of these cats was documented, it wasn't until 1960 that some fanciers decided to have these longhairs recognized for exhibition. Since some breeders had crossed Manx to Persians, the registries were reluctant to call these cats Manx Longhairs; thus, the name Cymric was adopted. Cymrics were accepted for championship showing in the 1970s.

Cymrics are active cats, agile jumpers, and good climbers. They are affectionate and intelligent but appear to be slow moving. Perhaps they are just saving themselves for playtime. These cats will reach a paw out to their person and ask for love, food, or water. Each paw touch is different, and their person soon learns the Cymric's language.

Cymrics could be referred to as the fruit bowl cat because their head and muzzle are shaped like a large-bottomed pear; their body is like a squat pineapple; their rump is round like an orange; their chest is firm and rounded like an apple; and their ears and top-head form a rocker that could hold a banana. This striking Cymric cat displays all those "fruitful" features. Kitty also sports an unusual red and white van pattern. Her powerful, compact body and conformation to type will win prizes on the show bench. The Cymric's muscular legs make this breed an excellent jumper.

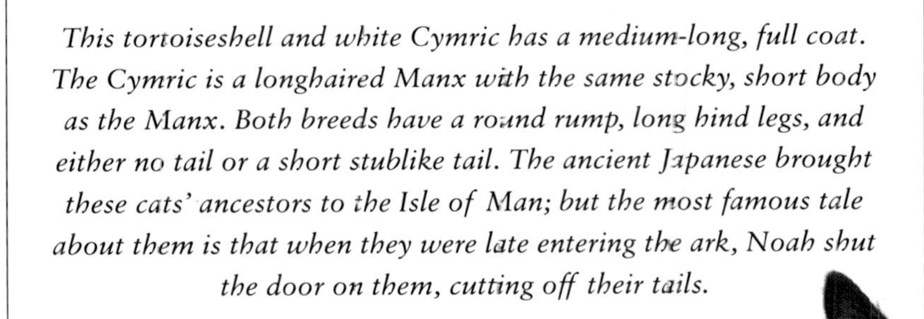

This tortoiseshell and white Cymric has a medium-long, full coat. The Cymric is a longhaired Manx with the same stocky, short body as the Manx. Both breeds have a round rump, long hind legs, and either no tail or a short stublike tail. The ancient Japanese brought these cats' ancestors to the Isle of Man; but the most famous tale about them is that when they were late entering the ark, Noah shut the door on them, cutting off their tails.

DEVON REX

An odd curly-coated cat was seen living in an abandoned mine in Devon, England, in 1960. This cat was feral and could not be caught. Interested cat lovers waited to see if any kittens born to neighborhood cats would display this coat. Soon a female cat gave birth to a curly-coated kitten. Kirlee was to take his place in history not only as the first Devon Rex cat but also as a new Rex-type variety. The Devon Rex has a fine, wavy coat that is thinner than the Cornish Rex's curly coat. These cats were recognized in 1967 and have admirers around the world.

Devons, like their Cornish cousins, are active, intelligent cats. They will run up to their person to give them a cat kiss and then prance off to play in the sunlight. They like to be held and cuddled. Pound for pound, they have more love in them than most larger breeds.

A young brown tabby and white Devon Rex poses in a pixielike stance. His bat-wing ears and short muzzle add to his impish character. This small yet spritely kitty is looking for new adventures and someone to play with. Although these cats are precocious and active, they love warmth and will take the time to curl up in a safe lap for some love. The fun-loving Devon Rex is affectionately referred to as the alien cat since he seems to resemble the alien character in the film E.T. *And this breed is just as enchanting, intriguing, and endearing as that little creature is.*

A black smoke Devon Rex appears to be an all black cat wearing a lambswool coat. The bit of white hair peeking through on his chest gives a grey cast to his fur. This kitty presents the well-muscled small body and shorter tail of the Rex breeds. Since the Devon Rex has a high body temperature, the soft curly coat feels like warm velvet. The unique but delicate hairs are all curled and vary in length and density. When this breed is in full coat, it is plushly curled like a small piece of lavish carpet; however, when it loses its coat, it may become almost bald.

EGYPTIAN MAU

The Egyptian Mau may be one of the only existing breeds to trace its ancestry back to the days of ancient Egypt; paintings of similar cats were found on tomb walls dating back to 1400 B.C. The establishment of this breed was initiated in the early 1950s when a pair of cats was brought from Egypt to North America. In 1958, the Egyptian Mau was recognized by the Cat Fanciers Federation. Breeders in Great Britain had crossed several breeds in an attempt to recreate the Egyptian Mau, but, unsuccessful, they imported a true Mau from Egypt in 1978.

Egyptian Maus are friendly to their person, quiet-voiced, and fairly active. While they tend to prefer single cat homes, they tolerate other animals and will deign to interact with them from time to time. These cats are affectionate. They request petting by rubbing against their person and then fall over to be loved.

This silver Egyptian Mau kitten could have come from the royal lineage of ancient Egyptian cats. Originally called the Royal Egyptian Mau, this spotted cat closely resembles a modified Abyssinian but has a less active disposition. According to legend, this breed was kept by the Egyptian pharaohs to keep the palace rooms free of vermin, to act as companions, and to help guard the children and young princesses. Unlike their cousins the Abyssinians, who could be owned by anyone, and the Egyptian Fishing Cats, who could be owned by fisherman, these cats were reserved only for the royal houses of the pharaohs.

EXOTIC SHORTHAIR

Although the Exotic Shorthair resembles the ancient Arabian (Dune) Cat, this man-made breed originated in North America. In the 1950s, American Shorthairs were crossed to Persians and the offspring were classified as Exotic Shorthairs. Since these cats were similar to the Persian ancestor in type and coat quality, fanciers decided to establish them as such. They were accepted for championship exhibition in 1967 and are one of the most popular breeds in the world.

Two shaded silver Exotic Shorthair kittens seem to be looking for someone to play with them. Exotic Shorthair cats are quiet yet frisky as kittens. They mellow with age much like their progenitors, the peaceful Persians and the dignified American Shorthairs. These two breeds were originally combined to thicken the coat of American Shorthairs and to produce silver Persians with good color. When they were mated, the resulting kittens were so striking that cat fanciers decided to promote them as a breed of their own. Sometimes called Easy-Care Persians or Persians-in-a-Clipped-Coat, these cats do not require the constant grooming that Persian cats need.

These cats are the "teddy bears" of the cat fancy. They are quiet and cuddly and enjoy sitting by their person. They do well in groups or as loners but demand their person's attention with soft-voiced complaints. They like to play with any toy that has a person on the other end, and they adore catnip-stuffed toys.

This red tabby Exotic Shorthair proudly displays the dense coat, compact body, and round head of a winning show cat. These gentle felines have a cobby body that resembles a rounded square, with short, thick legs set at the corners. Their massive head sits on their shoulders with almost no visible neck. Their short coat stands away from the body and feels like a plush pile rug.

HAVANA

Havana cats came into Great Britain and North America originally as dark-colored Siamese. In the 1920s, these cats were known as chocolate point Siamese, and it wasn't until the 1950s that the name Havana was used. Later, the Governing Council of the Cat Fancy changed the name to Chestnut Brown Foreign, but the American breeders retained the name Havana. In 1970, Great Britain changed the name back to Havana, and now this breed is recognized universally under this name.

Havanas need human companionship and crave attention. They do well in family settings. They are highly intelligent and can be easily trained. They are not as vocal as Siamese, but they are fairly active and love to play. Havanas are very affectionate and are shoulder clingers and lap sitters.

This Havana displays an excellent "corncob" or doglike muzzle that sets the breed apart from the Oriental Shorthair. The lavender cats that were originally produced looked similar to the Oriental breed and were called the Lavender Foreign Shorthair. Today, these lilac-colored cats stand on their own. The Havana has a lithe, muscular body with slender, firm legs. Their flattop head is longer than it is wide, and their large, upright ears are usually pricked forward. They have oval-shaped eyes that range from yellow to green. The Havana's short, resilient coat comes in either a warm, rich mahogany-brown color or a luxurious pink-lavender color like this kitty's.

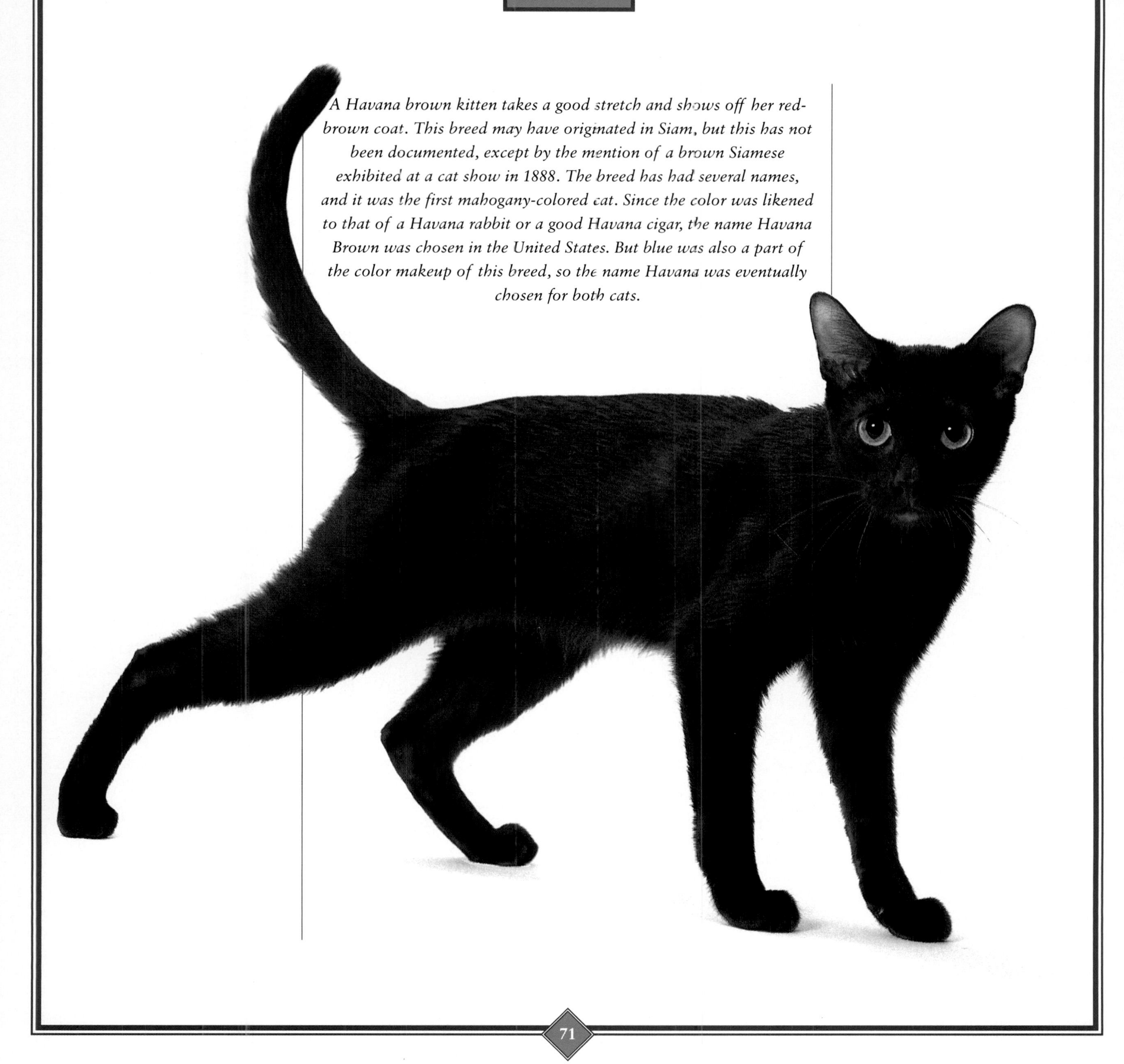

A Havana brown kitten takes a good stretch and shows off her red-brown coat. This breed may have originated in Siam, but this has not been documented, except by the mention of a brown Siamese exhibited at a cat show in 1888. The breed has had several names, and it was the first mahogany-colored cat. Since the color was likened to that of a Havana rabbit or a good Havana cigar, the name Havana Brown was chosen in the United States. But blue was also a part of the color makeup of this breed, so the name Havana was eventually chosen for both cats.

HIMALAYAN

The Himalayan is a combination of two breeds—the Siamese and the Persian. This breed originated in a genetics laboratory at Harvard in the 1930s, and Debutante was the name of the first pointed longhair. British fanciers decided that this lovely color pattern addition should be preserved for the longhaired breed. Colourpoints were recognized in 1955 in Great Britain and the United States with the other registries following. Whether called a breed or a color of an existing breed, these cats are here to stay.

Himalayan cats are sweet and docile. They have a gentle nature, are very quiet, and are devoted to their person. Although they do well in families and around other pets, they prefer to be queen of the household. They are not too active, preferring petting to playing.

Posing regally, this gorgeous red point Himalayan shows off a well-muscled, compact body, short tail, round head, and full coat that the top show specimen needs to be a winner. The Himalayan has the body of a Persian and the pointed color pattern of the Siamese. These cats are the legacy of genetic research conducted for color and pattern experimentation. The color genetics experts were attempting to put the point pattern on a longhaired cat. Fortunately, the outcome was a success. The resulting cat was so beautiful that cat fanciers decided to maintain it as a new breed.

The determined look on this Himalayan's face seems to say, "Will you pick a name for me already?" This beautiful breed has the distinction of having the most names of any known type of cat. It was originally called the Khmer in Europe, but after being recognized by the Governing Council of the Cat Fancy, the breed was named the Colourpoint Longhair. The American Cat Association also chose the same moniker, but other registering bodies gave it the name Himalayan or Self-Himalayan. In Europe, they are part of the Longhairs called Colourpoint Longhair or Himalayan Longhair. Today, in the United States, they are called Himalayan Persians.

JAPANESE BOBTAIL

One of the most ancient cats in the world is also one of the most recently recognized breeds. Bobtailed cats with unique markings appeared in Japanese art as early as A.D. 900. The Mi-Ke cat is a well-known symbol of good luck, appearing on temples and as statuettes in homes and businesses. This cat is Japan's first naturally occurring breed. It was recognized for competition in North America in the late 1960s and is gaining recognition worldwide.

JBTs, their American nickname, are quiet-voiced and very loving. They have strong family ties to their own cat family and prefer to remain together as a group. They are not happy as the lone cat of a household unless they are showered with affection and constant attention. They love to play and make excellent companions. Since they do not shed, they require little grooming care.

A black and white Japanese Bobtail stands tall and proud with his kinked tail pointing up with dignity. The unusual tail of this breed is not cut off short but gracefully curves around due to the misalignment between each vertebra. If this tail could be straightened out, it would be an almost normal length. The fluffy hair around the edges of the tail makes it appear similar to a bunny's pom-pom tail. These felines were favored by the ancient Japanese for their instinctive hunting skills. This reverence gave the cats the name Mi-Ke, and their likeness is considered a sign of good fortune.

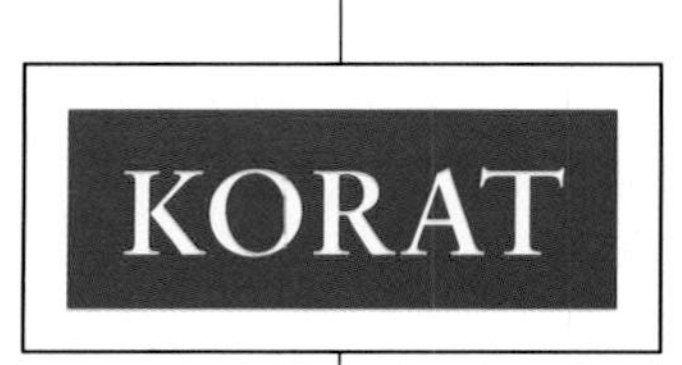

Korats are one of the oldest shorthair breeds, originating in Thailand (Siam). These cats were named after Korat Province and are called Mal-Ed (silvery-grey green) or Koklao (silver tip) in their native land. In 1959, two cats were imported from Bangkok to North America, and the breed was on the way to full recognition. The American Cat Association accepted the Korat for exhibition in 1966. Great Britain recognized them in the late 1970s, and they are now presented for championship competition in all registering bodies.

These cats are quiet, intelligent, and inquisitive. They enjoy playing with other cats or their person. They are perchers and will climb on a shoulder. They are very quiet and gentle and make loving pets. They are devoted to their family—cat, human, or otherwise.

A Korat kitten wears the glossy silver-tipped coat of this rare breed. Known as Si-Siwat (silver luck), Korats were held in high regard by the people of Thailand. These kitties were considered bearers of good luck. Ancient legend states that Korats were favored by the gods, who believed these cats symbolized all the attributes of the elements. Korats' shiny coat represented the silvery water and the earth's horizon, the white roots of their hair portrayed the clouds, their soft voice embodied the gentle winds, and their radiant eyes depicted the light.

This Korat gazes off into the distance, focusing his large, lustrous eyes on a desired goal. Perhaps it's a favorite toy, some tasty cat kibble, or a lucky person. The Korat is a medium cobby-bodied cat with a heart-shaped head, large ears, and a rounded tail. Their legs are angled in toward the center of their body, and their feet are oval-shaped. Their resilient coat is pale at the roots and silver at the fine tips. In bright light, these silvery cats appear to be surrounded by a luminous glow.

MAINE COON

The Maine Coon is a natural longhaired breed that originated in the northeastern United States. Although the exact origins of Maine Coons are unknown, they probably have some of the same ancestors as Norwegian Forest Cats. This breed was presented in the early cat shows, and in 1861, a black and white Maine Coon named Captain Jenks of the Horse Marines took top show honors. With the importing of Persians from Great Britain, the Maine Coon's popularity at shows declined until interest in the Maine Coon was revived in the 1950s.

Maine Coons are fun-loving and gentle. They are loyal to their owners and will patrol their home to guard against intruders. They have a quiet voice and talk in sweet chirps and twitters; they sometimes sound so much like birds that people wonder where the "songs" are coming from.

An odd-eyed white Maine Coon shows off the rugged beauty of this breed. The white cats in New England and Maine were called Angora until the Maine Coon cat was finally recognized as a breed. These cats have a large, sturdy body with a long, full tail that tapers to a tip. They have large, flattened oval-shaped eyes that are gold, blue, green, or odd-eyed. Their thick longhaired coat comes in all colors and patterns and was developed as a result of the severe New England climate. This kitty's silky coat, plush collar of fur, and fluffy tail serve as good insulators from the cold.

This brown tabby Maine Coon embodies the childlike quality of the United States' oldest breed. Affectionately called "gentle giants," Maine Coons are one of the largest of the cat breeds. Females weigh from 10 to 15 pounds, while the male cats can weigh up to 20 pounds. These muscular felines are sometimes referred to as Coon Cats. An old folk tale states that this breed was the result of a cross between a raccoon and a semiferal domesticated cat. Another story is that these large cats used to chase raccoons, so farmers domesticated the kittens to use them for hunting the wily, dangerous raccoons.

MANX

Manx cats were believed to have been brought to the ancient Roman island of Mona by Phoenician traders from Japan. Eventually, these shorthaired cats made their way to the Isle of Man, where they are now considered the national cat. Of all the breeds, Manx cats, along with their Cymric cousins, are the only tailless cats. They have been featured prominently in cat shows since the early 1800s and have been registered in the United States since the start of the first registry in the late 1800s.

Manx cats are quiet and faithful companions. They are interested in everything people do and are very willing to help. Their muscular hind legs provide them with excellent jumping capabilities; they can clear the top of the refrigerator from a floor-level standing start. They like to cuddle but are sensitive about their hindquarters.

A sweet, brown torbie and white Manx wears a thick double coat that makes him look soft and cuddly. Manx cats are the shortest bodied of all the breeds. They have a round rump, a broad chest, and large, expressive eyes. Their hind legs are longer than their forelegs, giving them a hopping gait like a rabbit. Although a mutant gene causes the taillessness, these cats can have several types of tails: A rumpy is a dimple where the tail would be; a riser is a fleshy area at the base of the spine; a stumpy is a small, stubby tail; and a longy is a full tail.

NORWEGIAN FOREST CAT

The Norwegian Forest Cat is a very old breed in Norway, where it is called Norsk Skaukatt or Scogkatt. It is believed that the Forest Cat may be the fairy cat mentioned in old Norwegian fairy tales. Norse mythology also refers to a cat, describing one so huge that even the god Thor could not lift it. Although this breed was first exhibited in Scandinavian shows in the 1930s, it was relatively unknown outside of Norway. American registries began accepting these cats in the 1980s, and they have now achieved higher international recognition.

The Norwegian Forest Cat is affectionately known as Wegie in the United States. These lovable cats make excellent companions. They are outgoing and adore everybody and everything. They are very quiet, intelligent, and responsible. They love to purr everyone to sleep, including themselves.

This young Norwegian Forest Cat wears a brown mackerel tabby coat. He has the long, soft coat and full, feathered brush tail typical of this breed. The Norwegian Forest Cat's long water-repellent coat was developed to protect him from the cold, wet weather in Norway. This breed is centuries old in its homeland, and many tales have revolved around the Norwegian Forest Cat. Legend has it that the farmers prized this intelligent cat as a hunter and in lean times would use the cat's hunting ability to feed their families. The farmers and the cats would hunt small animals together and then share their catch.

It wouldn't be too hard to mistake this lovely black and white feline as a Maine Coon, but he's actually another cold weather cat, the Norwegian Forest Cat. This breed's head is shorter and more triangular than the Maine Coon's. He also has thicker fur. This kitty shows off the excellent coat and body type of champion bloodlines. Norwegian Forest Cats are medium in size with stocky yet slender bones, good weight, and strong muscles. They have a moderately long body and an angular head. Their long hind legs provide them with their superb jumping and climbing capabilities. Their soft, silky coat has a rich, woolly undercoat

OCICAT

Although Ocicats bear a striking resemblance to ocelot cubs, they are a man-made breed that originated in North America during the 1960s. They first appeared in an experimental litter of kittens born to an Abyssinian/ Siamese queen and a chocolate point Siamese sire. One of the kittens, Tonga, was registered as a new breed. Subsequent matings introduced the American Shorthair to the ancestry providing the breed with a silver color. By the 1980s, Ocicats were accepted for championship competition.

Ocicats are curious and intelligent; they are strong enough to open most doors or cupboards. They can be trained easily, and they respond to voice commands. Even though they resemble spotted leopards, they have a sweet disposition and get along well with children and other animals. This affectionate, devoted breed can be a purring lapfull for their person.

A brown spotted Ocicat protects her silver spotted littermate. These kittens both display the sacred M on their foreheads. There are many legends explaining the M, but in this case it could stand for mau, which is the Egyptian word for cat. The Ocicat is believed to be a recreation of the Egyptian Fishing Cat, which is pictured on ancient scrolls and tomb paintings. This feline had a lovely spotted coat similar to the wild ocelot but had a much smaller and thinner body than his feral cousin. The Ocicat resembles both felines with his muscular body and spotted coat pattern.

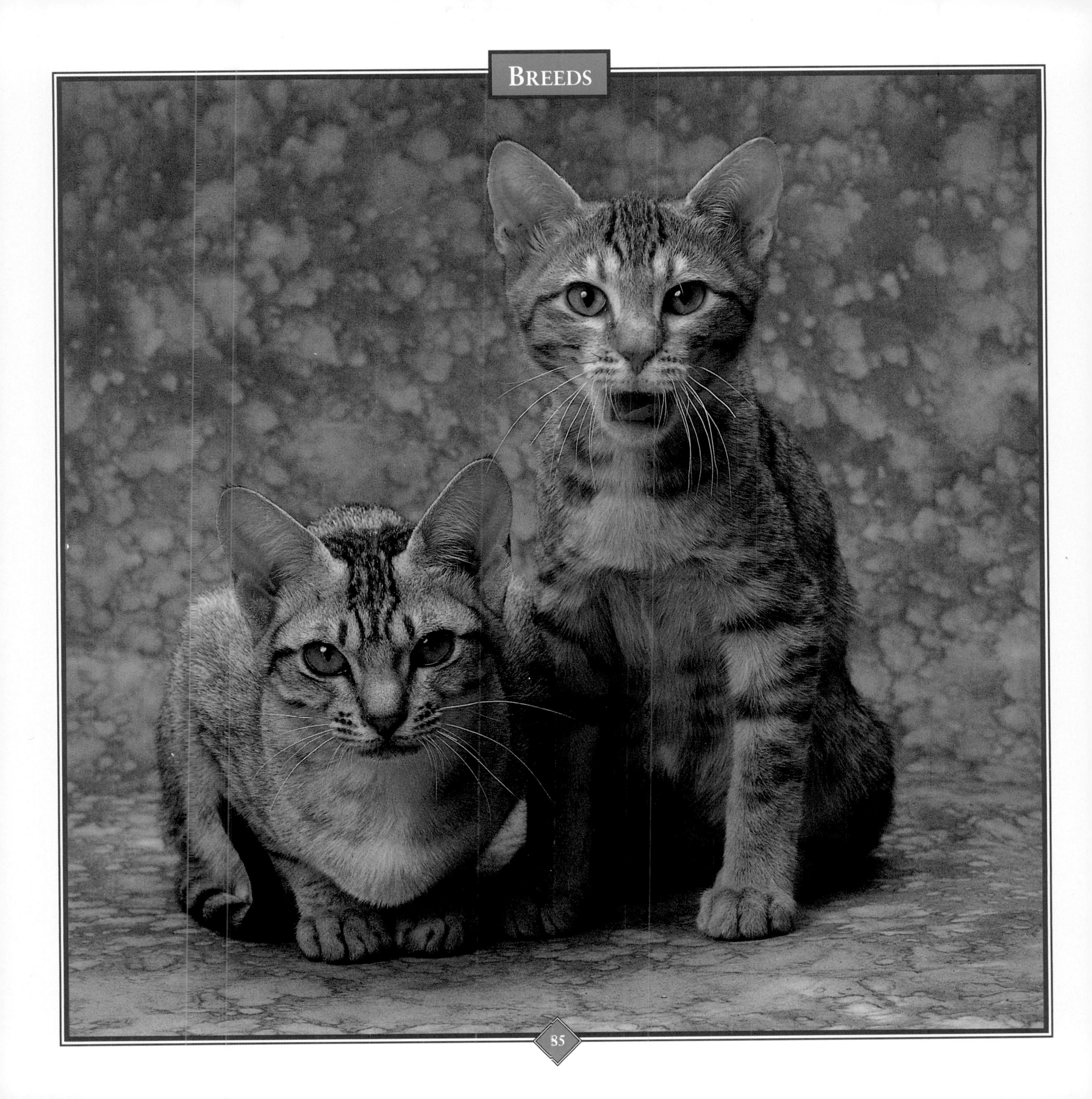

ORIENTAL SHORTHAIR
ORIENTAL LONGHAIR

This Oriental Longhair's silky ticked tabby coat looks almost as if it has been painted on. The glowing sea green eyes and smooth coats of the Oriental Shorthair and the Oriental Longhair give them the appearance of miniature panthers and leopards. These domestic cats were prized in the Orient. They were believed to ward off evil because of their skill as pest exterminators. They were called Silk Cats, and their likeness was woven into silk panels to cover windows and block doorways to keep the evil out.

Recorded history lists the ancient cats of Siam by color; the Singhasep was a bicolor of black and white, and other cats were black, brown, blue, apricot, white, or silver. These cats were exhibited under the name Siamese until 1920 when the Governing Council of the Cat Fancy eliminated all but the blue-eyed seal point Siamese. The solid-colored Siamese, excluded from the elimination, were the first of a new breed called Oriental. The blue-eyed white Oriental gained champion status under the name Foreign White in 1977. Although originally shorthaired, Orientals now come in longhair and shorthair versions.

These cats are as active and as talkative as the Siamese. They have an insatiable curiosity and are extremely intelligent. They can get into just about anything. They demand love and attention, and in return they are very protective of their loved ones.

Although this feline looks like a small black panther, she is actually an Oriental Shorthair kitten. Her gleaming coat shows off each muscle as she walks, and she proudly displays the long head, legs, tail, and body of this breed. Orientals are fine-boned cats with very long, slender features. They have an angular head, lean legs, oval feet, and a tapering tail.

PERSIAN

Two types of longhaired cats were recorded in the late 1600s—the Angora and the Persian (a stockier cat). The stockier type soon became the favorite, and the Angora lost favor to the cats from Persia (Iran). Most Persians exhibited at the first cat show in Great Britain were black, blue, or white. Gradually, other colors were introduced and accepted for championship competition. The Blue Persian was shown in the United States during the late 1800s and was the first Persian registered by the American Cat Association. Persians are the most popular breed in the world and, along with the Himalayan Persian, make up the greatest number of all cats registered, recognized, or exhibited.

Persians are quiet-voiced, laid-back cats that like to sit in secluded spots. They are happy just to relax and observe. While they are generally a calm and gentle breed, they do enjoy an occasional game with teaser type toys.

This red Persian kitten has the distinct privilege of being a member of the most popular and prized breed. As she grows, her baby coat will lengthen to the long, fluffy fur Persians are known for. Their woolly coat must be groomed regularly to keep it looking soft and beautiful. Persians have a short, thick body with heavy-boned legs. They have two head types: standard and peke-face. Both are round with a short, broad muzzle, but the peke-face Persian has a shorter, snublike nose that is set back farther in the muzzle. Their dainty ears are set far apart, and they have large, round, expressive eyes.

RAGDOLL

During the 1960s, a beautiful new breed was born in California. A longhaired, mixed breed cat gave birth to a litter of kittens with varying degrees of white on the points. People were eager to own these kittens, and those who were cat fanciers banded together to seek recognition for this new breed. Through persistence and dedication, Ragdolls were accepted in the late 1970s and are slowly gaining adherents in other countries.

True to her name, the Ragdoll has a distinct characteristic of becoming limp when held in a person's arms. These cats also earned the nickname "three feet of love" due to their affectionate nature. They like everything and everyone, enjoy both company and solitude, and are definite nesters. They are sometimes active and sometimes sedentary, but usually they quietly ask for love.

The deep blue eyes of this seal point bicolor Ragdoll express her gentle, trusting nature. When these cats are picked up, they relax all their muscles and become limp, just like a ragdoll. Supposedly, Ragdolls also have a high tolerance to pain. According to legend, the first kittens of this breed were born to a longhaired queen cat who was injured in a car accident. As a result of the accident, the kittens were free of pain or fear. However, many breeders say that the Ragdoll's pain threshold is no different than any other breed. Perhaps this legend was created to explain the docile personality of these sweet cats.

This seal point mitted Ragdoll's strong, straight legs add power to his walk. His luxurious coat appears to flow over his body like a silky robe. Ragdolls have thick, soft fur that increases in length from the head to the tail. Their coat comes in either solid point, mitted (white mittens on the legs), or bicolor patterns. They are very large, long cats with a muscular body and pendulous belly. These blue-eyed cats have heavy hindquarters, medium-length legs, and a long, full tail with a slight taper. Their broad head is a medium-size modified wedge that is flat between the ears.

RUSSIAN BLUE

LONGHAIRED RUSSIAN BLUE

The Russian Blue originated in the Baltic area. These cats were shipped from the White Sea port of Archangel to Great Britain and Europe in the mid-1800s. Originally called Archangel, they were also known as Spanish Blue and Maltese cats. Eventually, they became known as Russian Blue and were exhibited in early shows with other blue cats. Russian Blues were registered in the United States in 1900, but were not recognized for exhibition until 1947.

Although blue longhaired cats were recorded on the

This Russian Blue kitten has the captivating green eyes and plush silver-tipped coat that are the trademarks of this breed. The Russian Blue is an ancient breed originating on the Archangel Islands. These cats were valued by ship masters not only for their work as mousers but also for the "luck of the Archangel." Legend states that these silvery cats would bring good fortune to those ships that carried them—and they must have, for these cats were carried all over the known world.

Archangel Islands in the 1700s, the Longhaired Russian Blue, or Nebelung, had to be recreated by cat fanciers. This breed is still in its infancy and has been recognized by a few American registries.

Russian Blues are affectionate and so quiet that they are called "the silent miao." They love other cats, kittens, and children. They will rub their face lovingly across the hands, face, or legs of their person.

A Longhaired Russian Blue, or Nebelung, has an intense gaze riveted not on prey but on his doting owner. This loving breed is a longhaired cat bred to the shorthaired Russian Blue type. Although they were recreated by breeders, it is believed that these longhaired cats originated in Russia, possibly from the Siberian heights. Small enough to get through the nooks and crannies of ships, they traveled in these vessels around the world. Their long, silky fur made them prized possessions, and they were greatly valued as gifts. Both the longhaired and shorthaired varieties have dense coats that protect them from cold, damp climates, making them very hearty cats.

SCOTTISH FOLD
LONGHAIRED SCOTTISH FOLD

This brown tabby is instantly recognized by her caplike ears—she's a Scottish Fold. This breed's unique folded ears set it apart from all other breeds. The cat's ears crease forward and down, giving the Fold a kittenish appearance. An old tale explains the origin of these unusual ears. It was said that the howling of the winds across the moors and the wailing of the bagpipes caused these cats to fold down their ears, shutting out the cold air and the wailing music.

Born on a farm in Scotland, Susie was the first cat with folded-down ears. When she had a litter of kittens, two of them had this same type of ear. The white one, Snooks, was registered as a new breed. Many test matings were undertaken to determine the genetic structure of this folded ear. It was found to be a unique, benign anomaly. The new breed was named the Scottish Fold and was accepted for championship exhibition in North America in 1970. The Longhaired Fold, or Highland Fold, was produced from the beginning, but this variety was not recognized until the late 1980s.

Scottish Folds are loving, quiet cats that get along well with other pets. These cats are healthy and strong. They are particularly resistant to diseases and cold weather due to generations of natural selection among their ancestors.

A native of Scotland, this cat is called the Longhaired Scottish Fold or Highland Fold. Her flowing red smoke coat shows off the body conformation of grand champion caliber. Scottish Folds and Longhaired Folds are compact cats. Their body contour is similar to the British Shorthair's. They are heavy-boned, well-muscled, and sturdy in appearance. They have a round head with a short muzzle and straight nose. Both varieties of Folds come in any color and pattern. The shorthaired breed has rich, plush fur while the longhaired version has a soft, full coat. As with all longhaired cats, they require almost daily brushing to keep their coats soft and shiny.

Siamese cats date back more than 200 years and have an obscure origin somewhere in Southeast Asia. The ancient *Cat Book of Poems* from Siam (Thailand) describes cats similar to the seal point Siamese. These cats, who get their name from the country of Siam, were raised in the palaces as the royal cats of Siam. During the 1790s, Siamese cats were imported from central Russia. These cats were probably darker due to the colder climate or a possible mixture of Burmese. Siamese cats were accepted for showing in the late 1800s and are one of the most popular breeds today.

These cats are the "extra" cat: extra talkative, extra exuberant, and extra affectionate. They love everyone but can be very stubborn and opinionated when it comes to getting their way. They are climbers, perchers, and shoulder sitters, ruling their kingdoms with a velvet meow.

A blue point Siamese plays jungle cat among the plants. Active and fun-loving, these cats make up games to play and amuse themselves. Long and lithe, they are often called Spider Monkey Cats for their ability to climb, scramble, and cling to precarious things and Rubber Band Cats for the way they can twist, turn, and contort their bodies. According to legend, these cats guarded their masters' jewels, wearing bracelets on their neck, which gave them their long, elegant neck; necklaces draped over their shoulders, which created their long legs and upright, regal stance; and rings on their tail, which lengthened their tapering tail and added a possible kink.

PAST, PRESENT & FUTURE BREEDS

Cats come in all shapes, sizes, and colors with various coats to soothe each individual's touch. Certain types of cats are called breeds. While some breeds originated naturally from a specific country, most breeds were the result of careful mating procedures initiated about 100 years ago. Today, more than 100 different breeds are recognized throughout the world.

The first breeds of cats came from ancient Egypt where they were domesticated originally. The Egyptian Kephyr cat has been lost to history; however, the modern Abyssinian may resemble this cat in coat and body type. The Archangel cat of Russia was a blue cat that has descendants in the shorthaired Russian Blue and the longhaired Nebelung.

New breeds of cats are either being discovered or bred by cat fanciers around the world. In

This blue and white Tuxedo Cat is just one of many past breeds. This breed was presented in the United States during the 1920s. Unfortunately, the Tuxedo Cat did not gain enough adherents to become popular. Another cat that has been lost to history is the Dune, or Arabian, Cat. In ancient Arabia, this kitty was valued for its hunting skills. Today, the recently developed Exotic Shorthair bears a close resemblance to this historic breed.

SINGAPURA

Four unusual cats were sent from Singapore to Texas in 1971, one cat died and the other three reproduced. In 1974, their grandchildren went back to Singapore, and when they returned to the United States in 1975, they were registered as a new breed. Fanciers delighted in these small, ticked cats, and Singapuras were soon recognized for championship competition. Although these cats have been around for some time, they are still considered a rare breed. Eventually, their numbers should increase as more countries allow them to be exhibited.

These cats are quiet, gentle, and alert. Although they are shy and reserved, they are curious enough to meet new people. They are loyal and prefer to be with one person but have enough love for everyone in the family. They are nesters, and they have a purr that belongs to cats twice their size.

A pair of Singapuras displays the gentle nature of these cats and the excellent conformation to show specifications. The Singapura is the smallest of all cat breeds. They are somewhat compact yet lithe with a rounded head, short muzzle, and large almond-shaped eyes. Their short, brown, ticked coat resembles an Abyssinian's but is silkier. Singapuras only come in sable ticked tabby. This breed is native to Singapore and was known as the Drain Cat because these cats sought shelter and a place to nap in the sewers of the bustling city. Since mice and rats dwelled in these areas, the cats hunted them and thrived.

SNOWSHOE

These cats are a man-made breed that originated in North America during the 1970s. They have the characteristics of the Siamese with the white feet of the Birman. This new breed was developed by cross-breeding a Siamese with a bicolor American Shorthair to produce Siamese patterns on a larger, sturdier cat. These cats were called Snowshoes, or Silver Laces, and were accepted in the late 1970s. They are now beginning to be accepted outside of the United States.

These gentle, sweet cats prefer to be the lone pet of the household, although they will tolerate other cats and animals. They have a loving nature and enjoy children. Snowshoe cats are lap sitters and ask for attention with a demanding meow or a gentle tap of a paw.

A beautiful Snowshoe features the white feet and white markings on the face, chest, and belly that this breed is known for. The Snowshoe originated in the United States and looks like a Siamese with the white feet of a Birman. Although the Snowshoe is a man-made breed, there's a story that recounts the origins of this hardy cat. A pair of Siamese escaped into the winter snow and became lost. The cold froze their legs, bellies, and delicate noses, turning them white. After they were rescued, all of their kittens were marked in the same fashion and grew up with a tolerance and liking for snow.

Looking quite regal, this blue point Snowshoe has long, sturdy legs and a short, full coat. Snowshoe cats are medium to large with a muscular yet somewhat compact body. They have semithick legs and a long tail. Their head is a modified wedge with large, pointed ears. They have a straight nose and a muzzle with prominent whisker pads. Their walnut-shaped eyes are deep blue in color. This breed's short coat is semiresilient and may have seal, blue, lilac, or chocolate point colors set off by the cat's white face and feet. They are sturdy cats that love to be the center of attention.

SOMALI

A longhaired version of the Abyssinian, the Somali is a naturally occurring breed that has had lots of help from cat fanciers. Due to necessary breeding practices, the longhaired gene had inadvertently been added to the shorthaired Abyssinian. From time to time, these longhaired kittens would appear, but they were not actively used in breeding programs until the late 1960s. The first Somali was exhibited in Australia in 1965. The Somali Cat Club of America was formed in 1972, and the National Cat Fanciers Association accepted these cats as a new breed.

Somalis are athletic and energetic, and they like to play outdoors. They enjoy the company of other animals and children. These lovable cats are demanding of attention and will tap you with a paw or butt your head for a kiss and a cuddle.

An older fawn Somali has darkened with age but still shows the majestic conformation to type that top showcats display. Somalis have ticked coats like Abyssinians, but since their coat is longer, it has a rich, shimmering quality. They have all the characteristics of the Abyssinian. They are playful and very active as kittens and adults. Loving and interested in all kinds of people, Somalis make good "greeters," but they reserve the greatest love for their one person. They are intelligent cats and can use their dexterous paws to get into everything. Somalis love to be with their owner and take part in all activities.

This ruddy Somali tries to model the Abyssinian's Bastlike pose, but due to his long coat, he looks more like an inquisitive fox. This breed originally occurred in Aby litters. Recognized as a breed under the name Somali, it developed its own descriptions and designators. Called a miniature fox by breeders, Somalis have foxlike qualities. This breed's full tail, light muzzle, and longish nose peeking out of the full-coated facial hair resemble the fox's physical features. The full, silky coat of the Somali sports colors similar to that of the red and gray foxes. They are also know to be "as cunning as a fox."

The first hairless cat, the New Mexican Hairless, was bred in Mexico in the early 1900s. This breed died out because there was no attempt to perpetuate it. In the United States during the late 1950s, a hairless form of Siamese cat was produced and exhibited under the name Moon Cat; this line also died out. Finally, in 1966 in Canada, a hairless kitten was born to a mom cat with fur. This natural breed was called the Canadian Hairless. Eastern American and Canadian fanciers worked together to have this breed accepted; in 1971, Sphynx cats, as they are now known, were finally recognized.

These cats are energetic—they want to be in the middle of all activities. They are good group cats and like children and other animals. They love to cuddle as close as possible to their person. Their soft voice and gentle ways endear them to all who meet them.

These two Sphynx kittens, one brown tabby and white, the other pure white, can't decide whether to stay together or to try to find their owner. These cats have a well-muscled, medium-long body with a barrel-shaped chest. This breed has long, sturdy legs and a lengthy, whiplike tail. Their head is a modified wedge with very large, upright ears, and lemon-shaped eyes set back into their face. Their coat consists of a fine down, and they have small tufts of hair on the tip of the tail and base of the ears. They feel like warm suede and are often called Hot Water Bottle Cats.

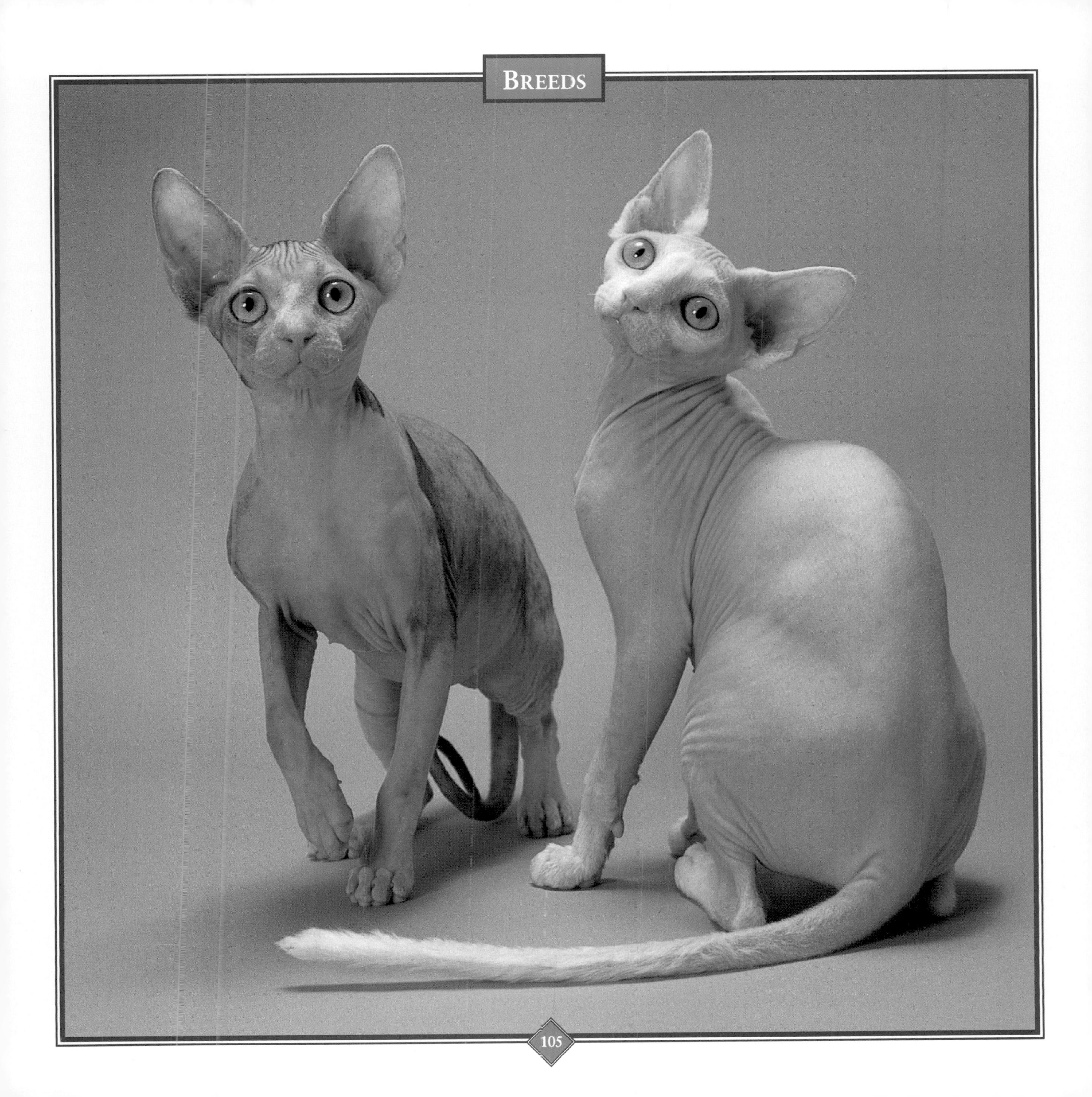

The Tonkinese comes in a variety of luxurious mink point colors, and this wistful cat wears a blue mink point pattern. The Tonkinese is a man-made breed that imitates the original ancestor of another breed. The Siamese was bred with the Burmese to produce a new breed, the Tonkinese. The forebear of the Burmese was a cat named Wong Mau, who was believed to be a Tonkinese. Cats from the southeastern areas of Asia were considered to bring good luck to those who owned them. Since the Tonkinese have two ancestors from Asia, they are considered Double-Luck Cats.

The Tonkinese is a man-made breed that was developed by crossing the Burmese and the Siamese together. In New York during the 1950s, this mating was done to create the Golden Siamese. These cats died out, and ten years later, in Canada, experimental matings were attempted again. These cats were first accepted under the name Tonkinese by the Canadian Cat Association for registration only. It wasn't until 1972 that the American based Independent Cat Federation, remembering the Golden Siamese, accepted them for championship competition. Soon other registries also accepted them, and they are now universally accepted.

These beautiful cats are very active and enjoy running, jumping, and climbing. They are outgoing, affectionate, and people-oriented. They have a great range of vocal expressions and will carry on long conversations with their person.

A platinum mink Tonkinese takes a relaxing stretch and displays the grand champion body type that this bloodline produces. This breed combines the striking points of the Siamese with the rounded contours of the Burmese. Tonkinese are medium in length, muscular, and lithe with medium-boned legs. They have a rounded wedge head and large almond-shaped eyes of a brilliant aquamarine color. Their soft, silky coat is somewhat short and lies close to the body. They come in the same point colors as the Siamese with the darker, solid body color of the Burmese. Tonkinese cats have a personality similar to that of the Burmese.

TURKISH ANGORA

The Turkish Angora, or Angora, is probably the oldest breed known. They originated in the ancient city of Angora (Ankara), Turkey. These cats were desired as gifts because of their beautiful silky, long coat and elegant, sinuous body. Turkish Angoras traveled all over the world, leaving their long coat as a legacy to their descendants. In the 1500s, they were imported to France and England but were eventually overshadowed by the longhaired cats from Persia and Russia. They made their comeback during the 1950s and were recognized by all North American associations by 1970.

These graceful cats have a gentle nature and do not like loud noises. They are playful but not overactive. They are a one-owner cat and are very protective of their person. Although they will tolerate other cats, they prefer to observe the other cat's activity from their own perch.

This elegant white Turkish Angora shows off a long, silky coat with a plumed tail. This breed has a slender body with lengthy, graceful legs. They are more dainty than the cobby-bodied Persians. Angoras have a long wedge-shaped head with alert, upright ears. Although the traditional coat color is white, their shiny fur may come in many colors They do not require much grooming care since their coat does not mat; regular, gentle brushing will keep their soft fur in good shape. They need plenty of fresh water and, like their cousins, Turkish Vans, may want to play in it.

This striking black cat with glowing copper eyes comes from the world's earliest, well-recognized breed. The Turkish Angora was the first longhaired competitive cat and is also called the Angora or the Turkish Cat. This breed's silky flowing coat has been its trademark, and it is the ancestor of most other longhaired breeds. Turkish Angoras were believed to be sacred temple cats as well as royal palace cats. Those who harmed this honored cat were punished by death. For a while, Turkish Angoras could not be taken out of Turkey without permission, and to this day the Ankara Zoo regulates the export of these cats.

TURKISH VAN

The Turkish Van was named after the Lake Van area in Turkey. In 1955, two cats resembling the Turkish Angora were observed swimming in Lake Van. The pair was exported to Great Britain, and their offspring are the ancestors of today's Turkish Vans. This natural breed is famous for its distinctive markings on the face and tail. They were accepted for championship competition in 1969 by the Governing Council of the Cat Fancy, but it wasn't until 1985 that the first American registry accepted them.

These striking cats are strong, agile, and intelligent. They earned the nickname the Swimming Cat because of their love of water. They are affectionate cats who like gentle petting. Turkish Vans swish their tails to express their feelings. They are loner cats who prefer quiet surroundings.

This inquisitive red Turkish Van just has to check out what is happening around her. As she poses, you can see the unique pattern that this breed is known for. This breed has given its name to the van pattern, which is now recognized all over the world as a separate design. Turkish Vans are much smaller and shorter bodied than their cousins, Turkish Angoras. They have strong muscles, a well-developed "swimmer's" chest, and medium-boned legs. Turkish Vans have a medium-long, sturdy body with a broad angular head. Their luxurious coat is semilong, and they have a medium-length full tail.

HOUSEHOLD PETS

Household pets are exhibited around the world in their own Household Pet classes (HHP) and make up one-quarter to one-third of American cat show entries. They have been registered since the 1970s and compete for Household Pet titles as well as year-end awards for Best through Tenth Best Household Pet.

They come in all sizes, shapes, and colors. Their coats may be long, short, or midlength with patterns ranging from all mixed-up to gorgeously flamboyant. From the mysterious black cat to the painted calico cat, each one has its own unique beauty. They meet their own standard—not that of a registering organization. In fact, the only standard they are actually exhibited under is "showing love, health,

This red tabby and white household pet surveys his kingdom and stakes out a sunny spot to take a warm nap. Up on this perch, he can keep an eye on his home. Household pets may be called domestics, farm cats, or alley cats. They may live in the country, in the city, at an animal shelter, in a safe and warm house, or in the great outdoors like this cat. These wonderful cats are the original fireside companions—the ones we choose because they are appealing and lovable in their own right. They come in all colors, patterns, and varieties as created by Mother Nature.

Two gorgeous household pets bask on a warm stoop in the morning sunshine. The calico sports a brilliant black and red pattern on his white body, and the cuddly cat on the right wears the van pattern with red spots on a white coat. Comfortable and assured of their place in the sun, they relax and guard their doorway.

and good care in the home."

Whether they are pedigreed or nonpedigreed cats, our lovable pets become family members. They are sometimes adopted from humane societies, purchased at the local pet store, or acquired from breeders. They may even be the stray cat that showed up one day and stayed for the next ten years. No matter where they came from, they are ours and we are theirs—and they know it.

This small "tiger" is a beautiful brown torbie household pet that has the look and the stripes of his wild cat cousin. Household pets are the cats without pedigrees or the ability to prove their bloodlines. They are the original ancestors of all breeds and the holders of genes that will produce new breeds and colors. These cats have their own personality, but they share the same charm, elegance, and feline mystique as their pedigreed brothers and sisters. These furry friends act as companions in millions of homes, giving us love and bringing us joy.

Chapter 4

Cat Behavior

Her conscious tail her joy declared,
The fair round face, the snowy beard,
The velvet of her paws,
Her coat, that with the tortoise views,
Her ears of jet, and emerald eyes,
She saw; and purred applause.

Thomas Gray — excerpt from The Tempted Cat

Meow, m'ring, mewuff! Some cats such as Siamese are more vocal than others, but every cat has something to say.

Contented, relaxed cats literally purr with pleasure. Purrs vary from silent vibration to motorboat rumblings. Meows are demands for attention and range from polite mews to noisy multisyllabic catcalls—the lower the pitch, the more agitated the cat. Cats typically meow to be petted, to be fed, or to be let in and out. Cats chirp and chatter when frustrated; perhaps an appetizing bird flutters beyond kitty's reach. Angry, frightened cats hiss, spit, and growl.

The majority of "felinese" is nonverbal. Tail talk, ear twists, eye blinks, and even whisker and fur position speak volumes.

Alert cats are wide-eyed, while slit-eyed cats are aggressive. Droopy eyelids indicate trust and mean a cat is relaxed.

This cat is darned interested in something, and he's not afraid to show it. His ears are facing forward, trying to catch every sound. Even his whiskers reach outward as though trying to embrace the object. With those eyes open wide, kitty is determined to see everything. The smoothness of the fur across his back tells us he's not fearful, excited, or irritable. In the next moment, this cat will either decide to get up and investigate more thoroughly, or he'll lose interest and turn his attention elsewhere. Reading the subtleties of felinese requires a quick eye, for cats rarely prolong their silent dialogue.

Uh oh, watch out for this cat. Can you tell that he's frightened? Don't push this puss any further, or he may lash out with a warning paw. For the most accurate indication of a cat's mood, look at the position of his ears. Confident, curious cats turn their ears forward so they won't miss a thing. But this little cat's ears are beginning to turn to the side like airplane wings. Flattened ears say he's both fearful and aggressive. But since his whiskers fan down and back in concern, and his dilated eyes say he's uneasy, this poor kitty is probably more scared than angry.

A cat has absolute emotional honesty: human beings for one reason or another, may hide their feelings, but a cat does not.

Ernest Hemingway

My, what big teeth you have! Cats open their mouths and force air out to hiss a warning to stay away. But this cat's curled tongue, forward facing whiskers and ears, and tucked forepaw indicate a sleepy relaxed yawn rather than an aggravated hissy fit. The cat who yawns in your company isn't being rude, he's saying he trusts you enough to relax.

But unblinking stares signify aggression, so never lock eyes with a cat. The ears of interested cats face forward to catch every sound, and whiskers are extended when they are happy and relaxed. Fearful felines flatten their ears to the side of their head, and they slick whiskers back against their cheeks. Vertical tails with the tip curled over are confident, happy tails.

Wagging tails and fluffed fur mean cats are in a foul mood; keep your distance from these testy tabbies.

There are as many feline personalities as there are cats. Introverts are the philosophers of the feline race. These cats enjoy solitude to ponder sunbeams, peruse the invisible, and meditate upon the world from window perches.

Extroverts are vocal, exuberant clowns. Always on the move, these kitties demand center stage. They are never mere observers, but are full participants in the game of life.

The shrinking violet is a demure, shy feline who

Even exclusively indoor cats may consider the front lawn or anything they can see from a window part of their territory, and this cat seems intent on something. He may be just curious, or he may be surveying his territory. Cats may become visibly agitated when an intruder crosses their yard, especially if the interloper is another cat. Kitty's ears go back, his tail starts twitching and lashing, and he may even growl and hiss a warning through the window. Let him calm down on his own, and don't rush to comfort him. All that pent up frustration has to go somewhere. He won't mean to, but since kitty can't reach through the glass he may nail you instead.

defers to all others. Although this cat yearns for attention, he has little confidence and hides and watches from a distance.

The independent cat is all bluster and ego. He craves human company, but considers lap sitting an insult to feline dignity. A soft, loving word suits this cat more than a caress.

The affectionate feline demands laptime, thrives on petting, and is a consummate neck hugger and shoulder percher. He doles out delightfully sweet whisker kisses and nose bumps.

The feline tail is more than a mere beauty accessory. The silent communication of cats depends to a great degree on the visual language of tails. Body language can be seen from far away, and tail twitches and positions are a way for cats to communicate without surprising each other. Kittens greet their mother and other trusted elders (like you!) with a vertical tail. Adult cats who feel confident in a particular area move about with the tail flagged high. A perpendicular tail is a friendly greeting between cats who know each other. Flipping the end of the tail is a cat's way of saying, "Hi there, how are you doing?"

One can almost see the little wheels turning inside his kitty brain. Feline intelligence is without question. Cats are great observers of minute detail and learn not only from trial and error but also by observation. Cats are often labeled as untrainable; but when a kitty wants to learn, he's a fast study and always remembers his lessons. Any cat worth his whiskers quickly learns where the tidbits are stored. If a stepladder is the best way to reach them, kitty won't hesitate to climb aboard. Educated cats know that manipulative paws can open cupboards and latches. When getting his way requires trickery, kitty's inventive mind is always up to the challenge.

I've met many thinkers and many cats, but the wisdom of cats is infinitely superior.

Hippolyte Taine

A telltale clue to a cat's mood is the position of his tail. A mere flick of the tail can relay a message worth a thousand words. A vertical tail indicates a friendly welcome, while an upright tail bent forward displays dominance. A wagging tail can signal ambivalence, anger, or annoyance. When the tail curves down and up, kitty is calm and content.

Gently touch this kitty's neck, close your eyes, and there—you can almost feel that purr of contentment rumbling from the page. Perhaps kitty's still tasting that tidbit of broiled chicken swiped from some unwary human's plate. Or maybe he's merely comatose with pleasure after being brushed by a beloved owner. Purring power varies from cat to cat. Some kitties are silent, and their purrs can only be felt. Others nearly rattle the windowpanes when their motors start running. Purrs are an expression of contentment and joy and are a kind of feline lullaby that soothes the cat himself as much as it does his humans.

Don't let this innocent face fool you. The cat's amazing repertoire of facial expressions and practiced posturing make him one of the best actors the world has ever seen. He uses this talent to his advantage to routinely avoid dangerous confrontation with his peers. By a carefully turned phrase of hiss and snarl and a meticulously timed flashing claw, kitty makes his point without drawing blood or even mussing his fur. Then with well-practiced mews (the more plaintive the better), kitty cajoles gullible humans into feeding him twice. A softly felt purr and a nose bump or two, then kitty's off to play with dream mice.

I could half persuade myself that the word felonious is derived from the feline temper.

Robert Southey (1774–1843), in a letter to his daughter, 1824

The grace of a moving cat is like a feline ballet. Walking on tiptoes produces the cat's long, elegant stride. Cats move their legs on each side together so hind feet tread silently in the tracks left by velvet forepaws.

A cat can go from doze to dash in a blink of an eye and is able to sprint up to 31 miles an hour. Tails act like rudders; they provide balance on tight curves and are used like a tightrope walker's pole when a cat traverses the heights.

Most cats are exceptional climbers and jumpers. They are able to leap five times their height from a standstill. Many cats relish lounging on the tops of doors or other high perches. One of the reasons cats are such skillful climbers is that they have no collar bones. This provides them with the flexibility to easily stretch out their forearms to the sides when climbing so that they can "hug" a tree.

Cats rarely fall, but when they do they almost always land on their feet. Incredible

This cat's slightly curved and raised tail shows kitty is interested in something—perhaps she stumbled upon a bird's home. While her tail tells us what she's thinking, it is also used as a counterweight when kitty is walking along a narrow, high perch such as this tree branch. As this cat peers forward over the branch, her tail moves in the opposite direction to reestablish her center of gravity. If kitty decides to make a quick turn, her tail will provide her with the stability she needs in order to make the tight turn onto another tree branch.

There is nothing more graceful than a cat in motion. The strolling feline first moves the legs on one side, then those on the other. If kitty is in a bit of a hurry, she trots by quickly moving one rear leg at the same time as the diagonal foreleg, then vice-versa. A dead run involves rear legs pushing off together with front paws still placed separately but quickly in succession. The feline poetry is spoiled when cats have to change direction quickly. They nearly stop before managing the maneuver, which may give dodging prey the time it needs to escape.

reflexes combined with inner ear balance sense and muscle control provide a cat with her remarkably quick reactions. In a split second, she knows which direction is up and how fast she's falling; she then twists in midair for a soft four-point landing.

Motion is never wasted, yet cats expend great energy in their everyday activities. Whether running, jumping, batting bugs, or pouncing on toys, daily play and hunting behavior are a kind of kitty calisthenics that help keep cats fit and trim.

Even grooming does double duty for the energetic cat. Adult cats spend up to 50 percent of their waking time performing some type of grooming behavior. Washing not only keeps kitty's fur looking pristine, but the twisting and stretching involved give her a real workout. Grooming also provides a stimulating body massage.

Cats sharpen their claws by reaching forward and dragging their nails over a rough surface to remove the outer husk. The repetitive stretching and pulling motion tones the muscles of svelte cat bodies and helps keep them from turning into kitty couch potatoes.

There is, indeed, no single quality of the cat that man could not emulate to his advantage.

Carl Van Vechten

The feline righting mechanism works in combination with balance organs in the middle ear and sight sense. When she falls, kitty first turns her head to an upright position, then with a series of twists and turns of her flexible spine, the rest of her body follows. But the righting mechanism doesn't prevent injuries. Cats falling short distances may not have time to turn and land properly. Cats tend to free fall and spread their bodies like parachutes during high-rise falls. But even then, the cushioned four-paw landing rarely is enough to prevent broken legs or a damaged jaw when kitty's chin hits the pavement.

She sits composedly sentinel, with paws tucked under her, a good part of her days at present, by some ridiculous little hole, the possible entry of a mouse.

Henry David Thoreau

How does kitty ascend the heights with such confidence? Her incredible sense of balance plays a part as do clutching claws and a tail used as a counterweight. Kitty's excellent climbing skills provide her with the perfect lookout—whether it's a tree branch, windowsill, or refrigerator top. This kitty's powerful hind legs help her move upward efficiently, while her forepaws guide her along the tree branch. Kitty is also at a great advantage at this height. She can easily observe her territory and hiss at any intruders. She is queen cat of all she surveys and rightfully so.

"Don't fence me in!" says this cat. The acrobatic ability and flexibility of the cat's muscular body turns every barrier into a challenge to overcome. Dexterous cat paws are invaluable in scaling the heights. But going up seems much simpler to cats than climbing down. For fences like this, kitty perches on top a moment, then reaches down the other side as far as possible before jumping down. Cats like to "walk" down vertical surfaces rather than leap from the top. In fact, cat claws are curved in such a way that tree-climbing kitties are forced to back down the tree they've just scaled.

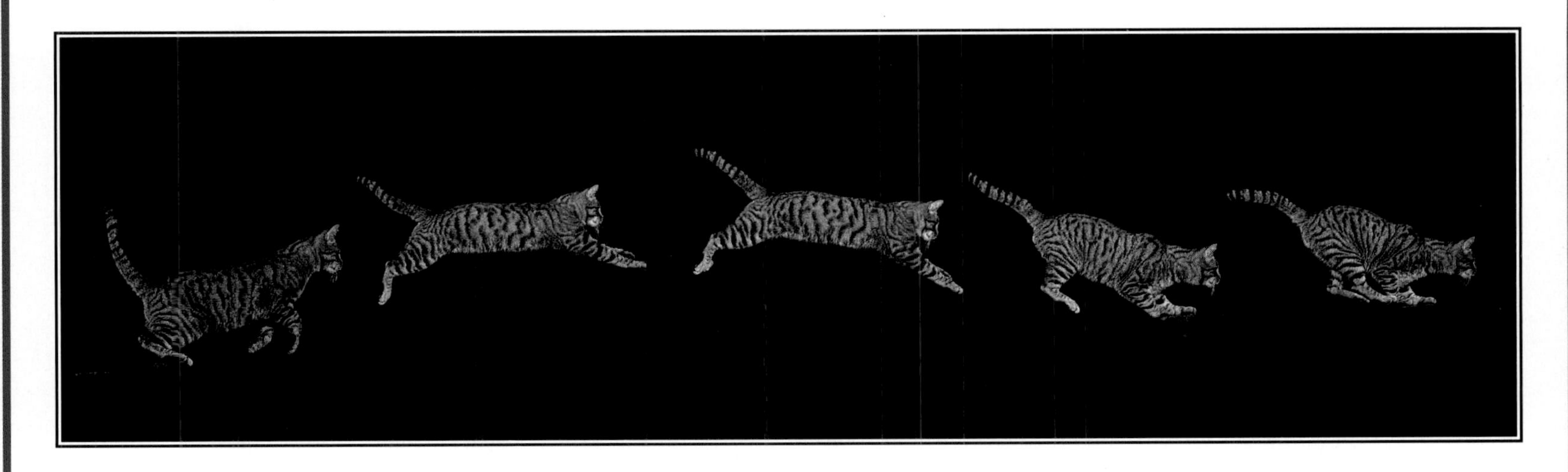

Above: *Oh, the sinuous grace—a cat hurls herself over objects with nonchalance, seemingly unaware of the intrinsic poise and elegance necessary to accomplish the feat. She runs, and without pause, she gathers her rear feet beneath her to launch her furry body into the air. Wind whips deliciously through the jumping cat's whiskers as she stretches through the air. She approaches her landing spot and extends her front paws forward. The spongy pads of her paws act as shock absorbers and provide her with a delicate landing. She has successfully accomplished her great leap!*

Left: *Every cat will take the necessary steps to get what she wants. Cats are nearly able to instantaneously and smoothly change their gait from saunter to trot or even accelerate into a furious run from a standstill. Kitty also has the ability to go from an all-out sprint to a dead stop and can freeze in position even in midstride. That proves invaluable when hunting, for the stationary object is much less easily observed than the one in motion. This cat obviously has places to go and won't allow a few stair steps to stand in her way.*

PREENING CATS

Since cleanliness is next to godliness, then cats have a special place in heaven. Cats are naturally clean and are meticulous groomers. They can pretzel themselves into bizarre grooming positions to stay pristine. Most kittens master the art of washing before they leave mom.

Some mom cats are so fastidious, their babies endure "wet kitten syndrome" from being constantly licked by her grooming tongue. But if mom wasn't a neat freak, chances are her kittens will be slobs too.

Cats comb their fur with kitty claws to unsnarl tangles and burrs. Scratching rough surfaces keeps front claws groomed; for the rear claws, only nail nibbling will do.

Some cats need help getting clean, and bathing is the only way. Many cats like water—if it's their choice. Owners of Turkish Van cats must latch bathroom doors if they don't want an intruder in the tub.

Cats love the grooming experience—whether grooming themselves, being brushed by their person, or having a kitty friend do the cleaning. Cats use their hind paws to scratch and groom areas that can't be licked, especially the neck and ear regions. But despite the cat's wonderfully elastic body, sometimes there are places kitty just can't reach. A lick and a promise from a friendly cat takes care of the problem. Kittens begin grooming each other and their mother when they are only three weeks of age, and this behavior continues into adulthood between friendly cats. Mutual grooming usually focuses on the head and neck—the most difficult places to reach.

Mutual grooming most often happens between friendly cats, like these Burmese brothers, and is more a social behavior than a hygienic one. Family cats often indulge in mutual grooming sessions and may purr and play with each other at the same time. When two (or more) cats are together by mutual agreement, it is common for them to lick and groom each other. Feline mutual grooming is a form of communication and often an expression of love and companionship. Kitty considers petting, from you, to be a particularly rewarding form of mutual grooming and an expression of affection between friends.

Opposite page: *Cats lick everywhere they can reach, then use a dampened forepaw as a kitty washrag for other spots. Kittens begin forepaw washing before four weeks of age. The fastidious cat licks her preferred forepaw until damp, then rubs the paw across her face and head, over and into the ear, across the eyes, and down the cheek to the chin. Then she switches paws and performs the face washing routine on the other side of the head.*

Left: *Cats use their muscular, pliant bodies to assume unusual and comical positions to wash hard-to-reach areas. A cat with a tongue like this seems able to reach nearly anywhere. Kitty spends much time licking her mouth, whiskers, and chin clean, particularly after eating. Then each shoulder and foreleg is groomed in turn, followed by the flanks, rear end, hind legs, and finally the tail from root to tip. When she finds a snarl, a piece of dirt, or rough skin, she uses her teeth to ease out the problem.*

With the qualities of cleanliness,
discretion, affection, patience, dignity,
and courage that cats have,
how many of us, I ask you, would be
capable of being cats?

Fernand Méry

Napping is perhaps cats' favorite pastime, and they spend 16 hours or more every day perfecting the art. A six-year-old cat will have only spent about two years of his life awake.

Rather than sleeping hours and hours at a stretch, kitty dozing is broken into long and short catnaps throughout the day and night. The feline mind remains alert recording scents and sounds during 70 percent of sleep. That's why he can spring from a supposedly sound sleep at the twitch of a whisker.

A cat's sleeping habits are extremely variable. No two cats are alike, and kitty may change his schedule daily. Nap time depends on a cat's age, how hungry he is, and even what his human happens to be doing. Kitty often plans to be awake when owners have time to pay attention to him.

Young and elderly cats sleep more than healthy

A sunny ledge offers warmth and an elevated view, both very important when it comes to choosing a cat bed. But one unwise roll, and WHOOPS—what a rude awakening! Why do cats seek out such unusual, interesting places to sleep? The first kitty criteria is that the snoozing spot must be warm and free of drafts. Second, it should be hidden away to keep their slumber from being disturbed. And third, cats tend to like elevation, the higher the better. That's why the windowsill above a heat vent or the top of a refrigerator with the warmth drifting upward is so tempting to cats.

adults, and bored or overfed felines tend to sleep a lot. In extremely hot weather, kitty finds a shady spot to snooze. Cats also tend to sleep more during cold, rainy weather.

Adult cats experience stages or levels of sleep. The first phase is a light sleep, or catnap, that lasts 15 to 20 minutes. The catnap then progresses to the next stage of deep sleep, which lasts for about six or seven minutes. Although adult cats continuously alternate between light and deep sleep, kittens fall directly into deep sleep during the first

Poor kitty looks like he had a hard day. Chasing mice will do that to a fellow. In fact, when cats are awake and playing, or up to other important feline business, they burn up an extraordinary amount of energy. Scientists speculate that may be why cats sleep so much at other times. Another theory holds that animals who hunt can afford to sleep more than if they were prey themselves. A successful predator like this cat, who spends less time hunting before catching dinner, has more time to spend napping. But these are just theories. Nobody knows for sure why cats sleep so much. It's just another feline mystery to ponder.

A sunny stair step is just kitty's size and perfect for sleeping. This cat doesn't mind that you'll have to step over him. In fact, kitty's worked out a great system; by sleeping on the stairs, traffic will alert him to anything interesting that's going on. Another good indoor napping spot is his owner's bed. With soft blankets to snuggle, no drafts, and your scent, it's the perfect place to sleep.

month of life. Kitty dreams are born during this deep sleep phase.

Nobody knows the exact purpose of dreams, but animals with the most highly developed brains tend to have the longest dreaming phase. People dream for one and a half to two hours each day. Cats spend up to three hours each day dreaming kitty dreams.

Although cats can't tell us what they're dreaming, they seem to relive activities from normal cat life. During deep sleep, the cat's muscles relax, he becomes hard to awaken, and his eyes move rapidly under closed eyelids. Although the rest of his body remains limp, the dreaming cat's whiskers quiver, paws twitch, and tail lashes as he stalks dream prey. A sleeping cat may meow, growl, and chatter at his visions.

Cats have indeed turned sleeping into an art. They sleep on their sides, on their tummies, and even upside down with furry legs sticking immodestly in the air. When short deep phases of sleep alternate with light sleep, kitty may continue to change his position. He starts on his tummy, with chin decorously resting on forepaws, then shifts to his side and curls his tail up between his legs. Soon, he's flipped onto his back like this cat with all four paws sprawled outward.

Windowsills are favorite napping spots for cats, especially if it's sunny. They relish the warm and cozy space as much as the nap. In fact, warmth is so important to cats, they may follow the sun in their sleep. Cat fur is such a good insulator that cats sleeping near a fire can singe their fur long before the discomfort reaches their skin.

These kittens cuddle together and enjoy each other's warmth as they sleep. As they get older, they will prefer to sleep alone yet still seek a warm spot to snooze. Some of their favorite places may include a laundry basket filled with towels, warm tops of computer terminals and televisions, and cozy dresser drawers.

Just like people, cats experience different levels of sleep. During deep sleep, kitty curls into a ball with his nose between his forelegs and tail gently curled about him. A cat deeply asleep is completely relaxed. A beloved owner whose touch and scent are familiar may even be able to lift and move a dreaming cat without him stirring a whisker.

What's better than napping with a buddy? Only friendly cats sleep together, sharing intimate space with a beloved companion. The concert of purrs lulls them gently to the land of dreams, while a warm, furry rump makes an extraordinarily fine pillow. When they're first born, kittens have no way of regulating their own body temperature; they rely on mom's warmth and piling on top of each other to stay warm. Cuddling with a friend must harken back to those carefree kitten days when it was a calm and secure feeling to sleep together. Only a rumbling tummy would dare disturb such tranquility!

CAT IN THE HAT

Cats start playing at four weeks of age, and the games continue their whole life long. Play helps youngsters practice and develop the skills they'll need to be successful adults. Games also teach cats important lessons about their world.

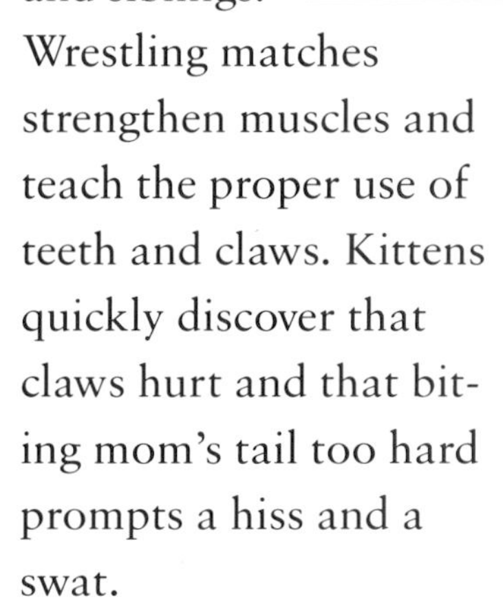

Playing teaches social skills. Kittens learn how to properly interact with adults and siblings. Wrestling matches strengthen muscles and teach the proper use of teeth and claws. Kittens quickly discover that claws hurt and that biting mom's tail too hard prompts a hiss and a swat.

Many cat games simulate prey-catching behavior. A bouncing kitten perfects the mouse pounce, and boxing teaches bird-swatting technique and paw control. Mom's tail twitching from under the door stimulates

"OUCHIE!" cries this kitten. Play fighting between kittens tones muscles, develops social skills, and also teaches kittens the important life lesson of how to inhibit their bite. These two seem to be still learning that last part. No matter how great the toy, nothing is better than having a brother or sister to play with. You can play chase and tag, hide and seek, and wrestle and romp, and there's other tails to chase that are easier to catch than your own. Best of all, another kitten will forgive an incautious nip or two and still consent to snuggle when it's time for a snooze.

This kitten may not know what a goldfish is, but she's sure anxious to find out. Inside that sly brain, she's trying to figure out exactly how to catch that enticing glittery creature without getting her paws wet. Cats can, in fact, become expert fishers, using a scooping motion to flip fish from the water. But mom needs to show this youngster the proper technique. Otherwise, kitty may throw all caution to the wind and go after the prize head first. And that could put a definite damper on the proceedings and put kitty off fish indefinitely.

When I play with my cat, who knows whether she is not amusing herself with me more than I with her?

Michel de Montaigne

fishing behavior as frantic kitten paws scramble and scoop to catch the prize.

Games of chase, hide and seek, and tag provide endless entertainment as well as rehearsal for stalk and pursuit of prey. Although some play behavior is instinctive, cats only get really good at it through practice, practice, practice. What a great excuse to play!

Cats learn about objects by playing with them. A paw pat is enough to send a leaf into flight, and batted pencils roll and skitter quite charmingly. But while a rock stays put when play is suspended, an unattended cricket hops away and hides.

Cats play for the sheer joy of it. Kitty is tremendously creative in pursuit of the perfect game and may even chase and

Playful kittens greet every day like Christmas. This Santa ornament is in for rough handling since cats treat toys as though they were live prey. If the toy doesn't wiggle, then the cat will make it move. A swipe from batting paws spins the Santa across the floor, and kitty gives chase and pounces. Having captured the prize, the triumphant youngster carries poor Santa around the room, flaunting her prey for all the world to admire. If Santa's brains aren't too rattled by the game, he may think twice before sliding down this cat's chimney next year.

What cat wouldn't relish a wonderful hiding place beneath the bed? Perhaps she's playing hide and seek, a favorite kitty game. Unsuspecting human friends who walk past kitty's lair are startled when flashing paws reach out and grab an ankle. Sometimes kitty's fascination with nooks and crannies gets her in trouble. Cats are caught between window and screen, and mischievous paws dump drawers onto the floor and open anything not nailed shut.

bat at invisible toys when the real thing can't be found.

Cats don't have expensive tastes, and a discarded box or paper shopping bag provides hours of cheap thrills. Some cats get a running start and then plop their fuzzy behinds on newspapers or throw rugs to play sliding games across slick floors.

Cats relish sneak attacks from behind drapes or from perches on the tops of doors or refrigerators. They love games of chase involving feathers, catnip mice, and the elusive beam of a flickering flashlight.

Interactive games with owners not only relieve stress, they strengthen the bond between you and your pet. Many cats enjoy games of fetch. Fishing pole type toys are great fun and entice the laziest lounge lion to get off her furry fanny and play.

PACIFIC
OCEAN
LONG BEACH
SANTA ANA
NEWPORT BEACH
RIVERSIDE
SAN CLEMENTE
SAN DIEGO
Reproduction of this map or any portion thereof constitutes infringement of copyright.

Opposite page: *Watch this kitten closely, or she could get into a world of trouble. Papers like this map are irresistible to cats who love to scramble beneath rustling layers and play hide and seek. Those car keys look tempting. What fun to bat them off the table and listen to them jingle all the way to the ground. Kitty could really have some fun with that pen. Cats seem enamored of pens and pencils and view writing as a game invented solely for their benefit. It's the unusual letter that gets written without the interruption of a paw swipe or cat pounce that steals the scribbler's pen away.*

Left: *The call of the wild rings true in this kitten's heart, and playing "jungle cat" is a favorite feline game even adult cats never seem to outgrow. The skills needed to successfully stalk, pounce, leap, and capture are practiced and perfected in every game. Whether hiding in the bushes or creeping beneath the dining room tablecloth, cats continue to invent new variations.*

Above: *This kitten has really gotten into the swing of things. Like most babies, she is exploring her world by mouthing and tasting everything within reach. Perhaps she's enjoying the elevated perch, and certainly it's fun for a teething kitten to bite that rope. She may even relish the gentle motion of the swing as it rocks to and fro in the breeze.*

Cats are despots, sad but true. In close communities, there is one top cat with no further ranking. Cats that know each other rarely rock the boat, and serious fights are infrequent. The dominant cat has usually been around the longest and has an established claim to the most territory. Kittens give way to adults, and altered cats bow to intact felines. If the dominant cat is displaced due to age or illness, squabbles may erupt until a new order is established.

Cats have strong attachments to a place and consider their house, owner, and even the view of the yard to be personal kitty property. Using both scent and visual signs, cats mark territory to warn off would-be trespassers. Marking can be troublesome when the cat is indoors. Cats back up to objects with a quivering tail and release urine to mark their property. When inside cats scratch furniture or rub-rub-rub against owners or walls, they're leaving behind

Kitty's finally managed to catch a mouse—why doesn't he go ahead and eat it? Doesn't he know he shouldn't play with his dinner? Actually, kitty isn't being cruel. Some cats may use such opportunities to get rid of their pent up energy. Cats also have a natural tendency to inhibit their bite, which they learned from playing with siblings and mom. Playing with live prey builds the excitement enough to trigger the necessary death bite. Other times, cats play with prey to gauge just how dangerous it might be. That's right, mice and rats stage fierce battles and fight back, startling the cat with bites that allow the rodent to run and escape.

This tabby cat probably isn't interested in a hug. More than likely, that Bloodhound has been poking his curious nose just a little too close for comfort, and kitty has had enough. Cats will sometimes initiate play behavior that looks like fighting. A pat on poochie's nose with claws withheld can either be a warning to "stop poking me with your snoz!" or an offer for further play.

scent from glands found in the chin, temples, tail, and toes.

A cat protects his turf by trying to scare trespassers away. He first threatens head-on with a wide-eyed stare. If that doesn't work, his ears turn to the side, his tail starts to swish, he bares his teeth, and he lowers his head. If posturing doesn't send the intruder running, a cat on the offensive will attack.

A defensive cat lacks confidence and bluffs his opponent by trying to appear as big as he can; he turns sideways and fluffs his fur. He sidesteps away from the threat with ears pressed low. His pupils dilate, he snarls and spits, and he may take a warning swipe with his claws. If the foe ignores the warning, the defensive cat turns tail and runs.

The urge to hunt is instinctive, but technique must be perfected if a cat is to be successful and actually catch

A cat fight is a fearful thing. Cats seem to know that teeth and claws can do enormous damage, which may be why physical battles rarely happen. Usually, disagreements are taken care of by hisses and flashing claws that are more show than business. After posturing a bit, one cat concedes defeat. When neither cat will back down, war is declared. Then the fur will really fly until one has established that he is top cat.

This cat's cheek rubbing behavior isn't scratching an itch, it's leaving behind a scent mark that identifies the object as kitty's personal property. The scent glands are found in the cat's cheeks, temples, chin, and even tail. When kitty nonchalantly wraps his tail around a table leg as he walks by or gives you an affectionate head-bump, he's marking with his scent. Scent identifies life for the cat. By checking these invisible guideposts, kitty "reads" the messages left by other cats and keeps tabs on the goings on of the world.

anything. Indoor cats delight in chasing bugs, but only learn hunting skills if mom teaches them. Mothers may bring kittens along to observe how hunting is done or may tote live prey home and release the moving target for her kittens to practice their skills.

When a cat is on the prowl, his body lowers close to the ground as he slinks quickly toward his target. Once near, he freezes and assumes the typical lying-in-wait pose: belly close to the ground, ears forward, and head extended giraffelike toward his prey. Then he draws near, one careful paw-step at a time. Finally within striking range, he draws his hind legs beneath his body with paws treading in anticipation, and he dashes forward to grab his prize.

Below: *Feline moms not only feed their babies and keep them warm and clean, they protect them from harm. Cat mothers defend kittens to the death. This little family makes a charming picture, but don't get too close or mom might turn protective. She'll rally her babies behind her, lay back her ears, and hiss a warning—don't mess with mom!*

Right: *The hunter nails his target with hungry eyes and ever so softly draws near, one careful step at a time. He may suddenly freeze in midstride and hold the pose with one paw hovering for several minutes to avoid alerting his prey. Soon, kitty prepares for the do-or-die dash. Then in a split second, kitty rushes his unsuspecting prey!*

Opposite page: *This black feline is displaying the typical defensive pose. He's trying to bluff his way out of a frightening situation, without losing his self-respect. Kitty tries to look bigger and badder than he actually is. He turns sideways, arches his back, and fluffs his fur. His puffy tail remains fearfully curled between his legs. Ears press closer and closer to his skull, and he hisses with outrage, hoping the brave front will force the threat to go away.*

REIGNING CATS

A male cat is called a tom and can become a father as early as six months. Tom advertises his macho status by marking his territory with pungent urine. He develops jowly cheeks and loose, thick neck skin that protects him from scratches and bites during scuffles.

If allowed outside, the tomcat roams far from home seeking romance and establishing territory, and he engages in fierce fights with other toms. The most ferocious male gains the highest respect among the fraternal order of cats.

Neutering dramatically reduces or eliminates tomcat spraying, fighting, and roaming behavior. Neutered male cats stay closer to home, become much less aggressive, and become more affectionate pets.

Intact male and female cats don't often get into scuffles because they seem to have parallel social rankings designated by sex, and they

This calico queen isn't shy when it comes to finding a fellow. During mating season, she becomes particularly affectionate. She rubs against everything in sight and rolls around the floor with abandon. This break-dancing kind of behavior, coupled with feline yodels, is designed to attract male cats from miles away. If they don't heed her siren song, she thinks nothing of turning into an escape artist and meeting them on their own turf. She may even mark objects with urine to arouse the interest of kitty romeos.

each have their own "home territory." In mixed households of whole and neutered cats, the intact cat (male or female) ranks the highest. When all males and females are neutered, it's a toss-up as to who will be top cat. The ranking feline is usually the one who has been there the longest and has the greatest claim to territory.

This handsome Maine Coon sire is already taking an interest in female cats. But a one-year-old boy cat like this one probably wouldn't stand a chance. He'd have to fight for his position among the other male cats and then convince queenie he's the one. Tomcat badges of honor include tattered ears, thick jowly cheeks, and a scarred face. This unmarked youngster is too pretty to have fought his way to top cat status.

A queen (female) cat may become pregnant by four months of age. The social standing among intact female cats is not nearly as strict as among toms. Each litter she has increases her status, and her rank rises tremendously among cats while she's pregnant.

During breeding season—typically from January to September—a female in heat continuously yowls, howls, and loudly proclaims her desire, sounding more like she's in pain than in love. Amorous behavior recurs every two to three weeks until queenie is finally bred or until she is neutered. Neutering puts a permanent stop to her interest in romance, including yodeling behaviors, amorous gyrations, and urges to roam.

When kittens are born, about 63 days after mating, queenie raises them alone. At birth, she licks them clean, guides them to her breasts, keeps them warm, and protects them with ferocious fervor.

The bond between a mom and her kitten is strong and is first forged by queenie's scent, rumbling purr, and soothing tongue. As the babies grow, mom teaches them how to use the litter box, wash themselves, eat from a bowl, and play. Free-ranging cats stay with mom until they are six to eight months old. If they stay together, house cats may retain close bonds with each other throughout their whole life.

Mother cats carry their young using the same inhibited bite technique that dispatches prey. Kittens grasped firmly by the back of the neck respond immediately by going limp. They curl into a comma shape that keeps furry bottoms from bouncing on the ground. Mother cats often move their entire litter shortly after birth even if they haven't been disturbed. Behaviorists believe this instinct arises from the desire to move the nest to a safer place far from the scents of birth fluids that might attract predators. House cats may play hide-the-kitten so much, they drive owners to distraction keeping track of the current kitty nest location.

The bond between a mother cat and her kittens is touching to see. This Balinese kitten seems determined to use mom's head as a perch. Like all mothers, queenie is imbued with an abiding motherly patience and tempered with common sense. She tolerates just so much before letting Junior know exactly what the limits are. Mom teaches her kittens all the feline social customs, and she instills discipline in the brood. Kittens learn the habits of a lifetime within the first several weeks of life. It's during these early days that personalities form. Just like humans, some cats become more gregarious than others. Kittens handled by people from an early age on tend to relish human contact much more.

CAT KITH & KIN

Kittens raised with other animals welcome these relationships as a matter of course. Adult cats learn to accept other animals if introductions are slow and kitty's feelings are kept in mind. Remember, it takes time to learn a new language.

While a dog's wagging behind says he's willing to be friends, a cat's flailing tail expresses anger and excitement. A cat throws himself on his back to ready claws for attack, but that's a sign of canine submission. A raised doggy forepaw invites play, but kitty raises his paw in prelude to an angry swat. No wonder misunderstandings occur.

The human/feline relationship transcends that of any other. We are part of the feline family, something like a beloved mother figure who provides food and who shelters her "cat children" from harm. If a person loves cats, a kitty returns the compliment without hesitation.

These Burmese cats share pillows in companionable friendship. Cats raised together often become inseparable buddies. They play together, sleep together, share the same bowl, and groom each other their whole life long. Other felines seem to prefer being the only cat and may not take kindly to a newcomer upsetting the status quo. It is possible for older cats to become friends, but introductions may take longer. Pairs of cats seem to get along better than odd-numbered groups. It appears that, when paired off, the odd-man-out third cat may be picked on by the others.

The cat and dog may kiss, but are none the better friends.

Anonymous proverb

Cats and dogs raised together not only tolerate each other, but they can become the best of friends. This pair obviously enjoys playing together and has mastered each other's language so there are no misunderstandings. Dogs and cats often enjoy playing together. Games of chase, tag, or hide and seek are always more fun with a friend. Eventually, they may even begin to take on some of each other's behaviors. Cats often learn to play fetch, while dogs try to climb trees.

Kittens learn friend from foe very early in life and take their cues from mom. But even older cats relish canine companionship. Differences in feline and canine body language can be a stumbling block for even the most gregarious pets. Just as cats rely on sign language, so do dogs. Signals get crossed when kitty doesn't realize that poochie's flailing tail isn't a sign of rage but a sign of hopeful canine camaraderie. When language barriers are finally overcome, deep friendships are possible across species lines. Dogs like this one will protect his cat buddy from other intruders, and kitty will protect poochie as well.

Cats and horses often become close friends. Perhaps kitty was drawn to the stables initially by the rustling, bustling mice who scurried through the straw and hay. Stable owners encouraged cats to stay and control the voracious vermin who pillaged food intended for the equine residents of the barn. But then kitty found another attraction—horsey back rides. Foregoing saddles for bareback style, cats discovered that a satin-furred back was both warm and high off the ground. Horses offer a perfect lookout and snoozing perch. And horses seem to appreciate the feline companionship as well.

The playful kitten, with its pretty little tigerish gambols, is infinitely more amusing than half the people one is obliged to live with in the world.

Lady Sydney Morgan

Chapter 5

Nine Lives, Five Senses

I am the cat of cats. I am
The everlasting cat!
Cunning, and old, and sleek as jam,
The everlasting cat!
I hunt the vermin in the night—
The everlasting cat!
For I see best without the light—
The everlasting cat!

Anonymous — The Cat of Cats

We've long been fascinated by the eyes of the cat. Although human day vision outshines the feline's, kitty's night vision is phenomenal. Cats can't see in total darkness, but they need only one-sixth as much light as we do and are able to use twice as much available light as us.

Feline eyes were designed for the hunt; placed at the front of kitty's face, they give her nearly 285 degrees of three-dimensional sight. This wide range of vision helps her to judge depth and distance accurately. Although kitty's a bit nearsighted during the day, her peripheral vision is quite sharp. She detects movement more easily than she focuses on stationary objects. Cats see blue, green, and yellow hues, but mousy-gray shades are probably more important than brilliant color.

Above: *In bright sunlight, this cat's pupils constrict to mere slits to reduce the amount of incoming light. The iris of the cat's eye is actually a muscle that regulates the amount of light allowed into the eye. It dilates to a wide circle in dim light but in bright light squeezes tight into a fine, vertical line.*

Opposite page: *This cat wasn't born with her gorgeous copper eyes. All kittens are born with blue eyes, and it takes about three months before they change to their final adult color. Kittens' eyes first open between the sixth and twelfth day of life. It takes another two or three days before they can see. By ten weeks of age, their sense of sight is fully developed.*

SMELL

Perhaps more than anything else, scent defines life for the cat. From the moment of birth on, cats use smell for identification, communication, and navigation.

Within a cat's nose are three to six square inches of a spongy, scroll-shaped organ containing more than 67 million scent cells. People have only 5 to 20 million such cells; we're scent-blind compared to our cats.

Two extra scent organs, the *vomeronasal organs,* are between the hard palate of the mouth and the septum of the cat's nose. Flehming, a grimacing, lip-curling behavior, transfers scent particles with the tongue to tiny ducts behind the upper front teeth where they connect to the special organs. Flehming is most often seen during investigation of sexual scents, and it falls somewhere between smelling and tasting.

Above: *Kitty thinks this cat mint plant smells wonderful. Plants related to peppermint and spearmint seem to drive some cats wild. When cats bite the leaves, they release the scent. The "ecstasy gene" that causes adult cats to enjoy the smell must be inherited. About one-third of all cats won't react to catnip at all.*

Opposite page: *When this cat was born, her sense of smell was already functioning. Newborn kittens smell their mother and literally follow their nose to find her. By about three weeks of age, kittens will have the highly developed sense of smell that already guides this adult cat.*

Although feline preferences for raw rodents would argue that many cats have no taste, cats can and do appreciate certain flavors. However, the taste of food isn't nearly as important as the smell. Cats are attracted to food by its smell; if the smell is satisfactory, they will taste the food.

The rough center of the cat's tongue has no taste buds. It's used primarily as a grooming tool and a food grater. The taste buds are found only on the tip, sides, and base of the tongue and inside the mouth and lips. Receptors on the taste buds make cats sensitive to the taste of water. Cats react most strongly to sour, salty, and bitter tastes. Proteins appear to activate a cat's taste buds, while animal fats are registered as smell sensations.

Canned food (and whole mouse) has about a 60 to 70 percent water content. Even though cats can receive most of their water requirements from those snacks, all kitties appreciate a sip from a pond or water bowl. Cats drink by curling their tongue into a spoon-shaped scoop. They lap the liquid, flicking each scoop to the back of their mouth and swallowing after every four or five laps. The rough center surface of their tongue acts like a sponge that also helps to retain water.

Cats are true carnivores who must have meat to survive. But even protein-loving cats relish veggies or fruit from time to time. Most cats don't react to sweet sensations, but a few go wild over melon or sweet corn. Grass seems to be a kitty favorite, and here, mom seems to instruct Junior in the fine art of nibbling. A kitten's sense of taste develops over time. The adult cat tongue is covered with rows of hooked, backward-pointing projections called papillae that rasp food and collect fluid. Newborns only have a rim of papillae around the edge of the tongue to help them grasp the nipple.

The eternal quest to find cat kibble that satisfies kitty's persnickety taste can leave cat lovers weeping in frustration. Food palatability depends on the smell, taste, texture, and temperature of the offering. The majority of cats aren't finicky, but even "normal" cats can be idiosyncratic. Cats often indulge in unique dining styles. They snub bowls of bottled water to lap from drippy faucets. Others eat with their "fingers," scooping water and food into their mouths with their paws.

HEARING

Extraordinary hearing enables a cat to identify and pinpoint mousy snacks, even from a distance. He can rotate each ear 180 degrees to collect and point sound into the complex inner ear. This vestibular apparatus also provides the cat with his uncanny sense of balance.

Humans hear, at best, about 20,000 cycles per second. Cats and people perceive low-range tones equally well, yet people can detect much lower tones than cats. But cats not only hear fainter sounds than we do, they outhear us in higher ranges. People can't hear high-pitched rodent chitchat at all, which is typically about 40,000 cycles per second. But cats can discern sounds up to 65,000 cycles per second. Kittens outhear adult cats, and sharp hearing tends to fade with age.

Cats can listen to more than one thing at a time, but this kitty seems intent on a specific item. Just as two eyes give the cat its depth perception, two ears collect and compare sounds in order to pinpoint a sound's location. Each ear is able to move independently due to more than twenty muscles on each side. Cats are able to locate sounds precisely even at a distance. Within an arc, they can find the origin to within five degrees, which means that at a distance of about one yard, they'll be accurate to within three inches.

The cat has a nervous ear,
that turns this way and that
And what the cat may hear,
is known but to the cat.
David Morton

Maybe this kitty hears his favorite sound—the sound of a can opener. His brain can instantaneously process this familiar sound, and he can react accordingly. The external portion of the cat's ear, called the pinna, locates and collects sound waves and funnels them downward into the inner workings. Here, the sound impacts a taut membrane called the ear drum, which passes the vibration on to a complex chain of tiny vibrating bones and fluid-filled tubes. These connect to the auditory nerve, which speeds the message on to the brain for translation.

TOUCH

The cat's sense of touch is not only a protective mechanism, it's one of the most pleasurable sensations for the cat. Cats love sunbathing, mutual grooming, and stroking and cuddling by a special human.

Paw pads and nose leather are the most sensitive to touch. With them, cats can tell differences in temperature as slight as one or two degrees. Cats like heat so much they may singe whiskers or tail fur before reacting with discomfort.

Kitty doesn't need direct contact to feel something. Scattered beneath the cat's skin all over her body are tiny pressure pads. They alert the cat if even a single hair is disturbed. Whiskers set deep into the skin act like antennae and help a cat judge distances between objects and even detect changes in air pressure.

The spread of a cat's whiskers is approximately the same as the width of her body. The thick wirelike hairs sprout from her cheeks, chin, eyebrows, and even the backs of her front legs. Called vibrissae, *these specialized hairs are arranged in patterns as unique as fingerprints. Whiskers act as feelers to help her judge whether she'll fit through tight openings. At night when there's not enough light to see, kitty uses her whiskers to feel her way around. Kitty doesn't even need whisker contact with objects to detect them since her whiskers can recognize subtle changes in air current and atmospheric pressure.*

Below: *Cats have receptors that detect heat and cold all over their body. This cat is basking in the warmth of a delightful sunbath. The sun's caress and the sensation of touch are not only pleasurable, but practical as well. At birth, blind and deaf kittens rely greatly on touch to keep them in contact with their mother. Her rough, massaging tongue and the vibrations of her purrs signal that all is well. Later as adults, cats seek out a favorite human's gentle hand just as they did their mother's ministering touch.*

Cats touch each other as a means of bonding and establishing their hierarchy. A nose-to-nose greeting between friendly cats is a sign of affection. Touch is an important part of normal socialization for cats. Kittens that have no contact with people have a difficult time becoming affectionate pets. Kittens handled on a daily basis not only bond strongly with humans, they improve their learning ability.

SIXTH SENSE

The extraordinary sensory ability cats possess has for years made them seem supernatural. Stories abound of psychic cats predicting weather changes, earthquakes, and other events. Kitties who find their way home over extraordinary distances prompt shivers of awe and amazement.

In fact, keen senses of smell, hearing, and touch enable cats to detect changes in barometric pressure, distant thunder, or other weather cues humans miss. Kitty's sensitivity to vibration and magnetic fields may explain how he predicts earthquakes. And his homing ability is thought to be due to magnetized iron deposits in his brain that act like an internal compass.

A cat's acute senses combined with his meaningful expressions reinforce our belief that cats do indeed have extrasensory perceptions. But despite hopeful theories, some things remain beyond our understanding. The cat's wondrous sixth sense remains a magical mystery to us.

Does that gaze penetrate beyond the veil of time? The ancient Egyptians thought so and named the cat Mau, which means the seer. According to folklore, calico cats have the gift of second sight. Tricolor cats were believed to protect the house where they lived from being destroyed by fire. All cats at one time were thought to be able to predict the weather, good fortune, or even tragedy. Even in modern times, the cat's seeming clairvoyance has been linked to an inexplicable sixth sense. One published account tells of a cat who meowed frantically for his owner to follow him, then led his owner far away to a strange house. There, the cat's kitten-friend lay mortally wounded, having just been hit by a car.

Chapter 6

They Never Come When You Call Them

Our old cat has kittens three,
And what do you think their names shall be?
Pepper-pot, Sootkins, Scratch-away,—there!
Was there ever a kitten with these to compare?
And we call their old mother, now what do you think?
Tabitha Long-Claws Tiddley-Wink!

Thomas Hood — Tabitha Long-Claws Tiddley-Wink

THE NAME GAME

Naming is a serious business that cannot be taken lightly. An inappropriate name bruises kitty feelings as much (or more!) than physical injury. Cats may not be fluent in human-speak, but they understand intent. A positive name promotes self-esteem in the cat, while a hateful name fosters depression or even nastiness. Cats must be christened to celebrate their glorious feline spirit, and a name must complement the individual cat.

Cats are named for appearance (Blackie), for where they were adopted (Freeway), for personality (Bravado), and even in honor of others (Elvis). Obscure names tell less obvious stories: Solo isn't a loner, but was named for the gas station where he was found; and lovable Shirin was named so because her name means sweet in Persian.

Whether obvious or subtle, it is the cat herself who ultimately chooses to accept and answer to a name—or not.

According to a 1994 survey, the most popular names for cats, in order, were: Kitty, Smokey, Tigger, Tiger, Max, Patches, Missy, Shadow, Samantha—and tied for 10th were Baby, Callie, and Midnight. But Junior seems fitting for this precocious youngster. Even though the other cats aren't there, names tell us what they look like, their ages, and even some of their idiosyncrasies.

It would seem from the names listed on the bowls that three kitty generations are represented—Gramps, Mama Cat, and Junior. Whiskers probably has luxurious ones, while one would expect Jumbo to tip the scales on the high side. Names certainly paint a picture of the individual.

They say the test of this is whether a man can write an inscription. I say, "Can he name a kitten?" And by this test I am condemned, for I cannot.

Samuel Butler

THEY WEAR IT WELL

Cats often sport names that describe their good looks. Orange or yellow cats go by Rusty, Pumpkin, and Ginger. From light to dark, cats answer to Snowball or Cotton, Smokey or Smudge, and Midnight or Ebony.

Distinctive markings also get their due. Batman and Bandit are masked, Groucho doesn't shave, while Mittens, Boots, and Spats wear striking "paw gear." Patches is a calico, whereas Oreo and Tux are black and white.

Cat names point out physical features as well. Big Foot and Digit have extra toes, and a three-legged cat is often called Tripod. The names Scruffy, Suede, and Pixie describe three very different cats: a shaggy cat, a Sphynx cat, and a small cat. And of course, there's the ever popular cat name Fluffy, which aptly describes our cuddly felines.

Even though an Abyssinian cat is usually on the move, this one has slowed down to take a nap in the sunlight. This cat's coat color may prompt names like Megan (from the color of nutmeg), Cinnamon, or Amber. For Abyssinian extroverts, the names Spice or Ginger Snap would comment on both personality and looks, but a name like Sunshine might be better suited for this Aby. Other cats are named less for appearance and more for the way they act. Twin cats were named Goodness and Mercy after the Bible verse that says, "Surely, goodness and mercy shall follow me." And they do.

The gorgeous fur of this beauty begs the name Tala, which is Persian for gold. He could also be called Whiskers since he sports a bold set. Ruff, Fluff, or Puff also work well for this fuzzy furball, as does the name Topaz for those stunning eyes. One cat was named Irish because he was born on St. Patrick's Day—and he was a redhead. But cats are often named for appearance other than color. Six-Pack was so named because he had six toes, and a cat named Bunny had a powder-puff tail.

Here's a kitty intent on playing king of the rock—is his name Rex? With those distinctive markings, perhaps this cat should be called Tabby. Equally appropriate are Spot, Dottie, Tiger, or Tigger, and that tail might conjure a name like 'Coon. Should your imagination really run wild, you could comment on this cat's striking eye markings by choosing the name Maybelline. The feral look of this cat also makes monikers like Simba, Sheena, Lynx, or Cheetah appropriate. That plush, soft fur might inspire the cat to be called Velvet. Every cat's appearance suggests a number of appropriate names.

Opposite page: *The beauty of this gray and white feline offers several obvious possibilities for a name: Shadow, Smokey, or even Kingsford (for the charcoal). One cat was named 50/50 because half his face was gray and the other side was white. This cat's white markings call for a name such as Bib or Bootsy. The gray mark alongside his nose also makes him a candidate for Smudge.*

*A cat is there when you call her—
if she doesn't have
something better to do.*
Bill Adler

This cat's luxurious fur seems to flow like gray Silk. Perhaps she's called Satin or Flossy? When she moves, does she float like wafting Mist? Or does she seem more like a Ghost or a Sprite that passes in a silent, swift rush through the hours of Dusk or Twilight? Any of these names might suit her, but perhaps the best name of all would be Keely, which is the Gaelic word for beautiful.

NAMES OF CELEBRITIES' CATS

A proper name reflects the feline soul and is always rich in meaning. Celebrities' cats named for their looks include President Clinton's cat Socks and Roosevelt's six-toed cat Slippers. When actress Janet Leigh adopted a tiny white kitten, the baby looked so much like holiday leftovers she named the cat Turkey.

Cats are also named to honor others. Katie and Robert Wagner's cats Moon and Dweezil were gifts from Dweezil and Moon Unit Zappa, musician Frank Zappa's son and daughter. Robert Goulet calls his Siamese cat Wart, which was the nickname of the young King Arthur. Chopin was the name of author F. Scott Fitzgerald and his wife Zelda's white Persian cat, honoring the composer Frederic Chopin. Charles Dickens was also a great cat lover and named his cat William. Dickens later discovered that the name Williamina was more appropriate for his cat.

This kitten-toting gentleman is none other than Samuel Clemens, commonly known as Mark Twain. Twain had a deep and abiding love and respect for cats and often referred to them in his writing. He gave his cats tongue-twisting monikers to help children practice pronunciation. At one time, he shared his house with cats named Buffalo Bill, Beelzebub, Blatherskit, and Apollinaris. Twain's property adjoined that of author Harriet Beecher Stowe, who wrote Uncle Tom's Cabin. *She also loved and cherished her cats. Since the two sets of felines often visited each other, the authors had the cats "write" letters to each other.*

Such was Seraphita, and never did cat more amply justify a poetic name . . .

Théophile Gautier, French Writer

Betty White has been a pet lover her whole life. She found this stunning black cat hanging out in her backyard shortly after her husband, Allen Ludden, passed away. But the cat vanished if she so much as looked at it. The cat seemed fascinated by Timmy, her little black poodle. Eventually, the homeless cat started accepting food from Betty. Then one day the stray kitty followed Timmy inside. It took a long time to win the cat's trust, but Timmy eventually made friends with the black cat. Betty promptly adopted the feline and named him T. K. for Timmy's Kitty.

"ARISTOCAT" NAMES

Showcats sport names that dazzle the senses. Names are registered to keep track of kitty's genealogy or pedigree, so every name must be different. Names often employ unique spellings to avoid duplicating those already in use.

First names are usually the cattery where kitty was born and describe a particular breed. Earmark cattery breeds Scottish Folds, Abyriginal is home to Abyssinians, and Rumplestump Manx produces tailless wonders. Then come the ingenious individual names. From Cashmere Critter (Chartreux) to Diva's Lunatic Fringe (Abyssinian), names speak volumes about each cat's looks and personality.

The complete registered name can be a tongue-twister describing the cat's ancestry, attitude, and appearance. Allmykittens Bluedahlia Mysterymain is a blue patched tabby and white Maine Coon. A Japanese Bobtail goes by

Perhaps no other breed prompts more innovative and entertaining names than the nearly hairless Sphynx. Skin with a fine hair coat that feels like suede leaves little to the imagination in the way of body shape. Names like Plush, Velvet, or even Peach Fuzz come to mind, as do Pixie, Gremlin, and Gnome. One group of Sphynx kittens were named, respectively, Piccard, Scantilly Clad, Cowboy, Popeye, Shaman, Chunky Chip, Harley Quinn, and Pearlie Mae Bailey. Another Sphynx cat's registered name is Bijou Iron Meow't—wouldn't that hurt?!

The cat has nine lives: Three for playing, three for straying, three for staying.

English proverb

Maternity doesn't mellow the cat; maturity comes with age, whether a cat has babies or not. Actually, having kittens increases her risk for several health problems.

The Altering Myth: Altering is said to create fat, lazy cats that won't hunt. But cats who craved mousy morsels in the past will continue to indulge their taste buds. Altering does stem romantic exertions, and if amorous adventures were kitty's sole exercise, she may turn pudgy if new kitty calisthenics aren't performed.

The Baby Myth: The ancient myth that cats steal the breath from babies arose from the Hebrew tale of Adam's first wife, Lilith. Lilith fled Eden and became a vampire who could assume the form of a huge black cat called El Broosha. Human newborns were El Broosha's favorite prey.

Today, we know that cats go nose to nose with an infant to smell milky breath, and kitty nose bumps are a sign of feline affection. Cats are so intensely alert to change that some bump noses with a baby if they notice something different. Concerned (yet uninformed) parents who find kitty nose to nose with a baby endorse the myth as truth when in fact kitty was probably only reacting to the infant's kitten-like cries.

Several myths exist regarding black cats. Since black was considered the color of evil, and cats were thought to belong to the devil, black cats were doubly doomed. Therefore, a black cat crossing one's path was a bad omen. But not all black cat myths were bad. Passing the tail or a single hair from the tail of a black cat over an afflicted eye was said to cure everything from a sty to blindness. Some people superstitiously kept and protected black cats, believing this courtesy to Satan's favored animal would keep him off their back and help them prosper.

A cat can be trusted to purr when she is pleased, which is more than can be said for human beings.

William Ralph Inge

"White cats make bad mothers." Oh, really? Certainly, many white cats make very fine mothers, but this myth probably has some factual basis. Some white cats are born with a congenital hearing loss that results in deafness. Such cats wouldn't be able to hear kittens cry, which may be how the myth started. Deafness is usually associated with blue-eyed white cats, like this one; those with one blue eye may be deaf only on that side. The condition touches about one in five white cats; longhaired cats are affected more often than shorthaired cats. Deaf cats, however, can lead happy, productive lives.

LORE

The customs, whimsy, and enigmatic rituals of the feline race have fascinated, amused, and confounded humankind for centuries. In some instances, we are no closer to understanding, and we can only wonder why and how kitty does what he does.

The Purr: Ah, the mysterious purr . . . deceptively simple yet gloriously uplifting, the purr is a soothing mantra to both human and feline souls. Vibrating purrs are an endearing means of feline communication. They are used to instruct kittens, to cement the bonds of friendship, and to calm self or companions. The purring cat song is an expression of overwhelming emotion; when kitty can no longer contain his joy, fury, contentment, or even pain, he bubbles over in purrs that vibrate from throat and chest throughout his entire body.

How do cats purr? Some say a cat's vestibular

This kitty seems to be having a wonderful time scratching his back in the dirt. Why do cats throw themselves before you on the ground, like an offering of fish before the great cat deity? Presenting his unprotected tummy is an incredible compliment that indicates trust. Translated from felinese, this behavior says either, "Please play with me," or "Wouldja pet me and groom me?" And of course, it would be terribly impolite if one didn't accommodate the cat.

This orange cat seems intent on something just out of reach. That wonderful sense of balance comes in handy when cats hop up on their hind legs to greet you. Cats turn into impatient hind-leg walkers to improve the view and increase their access to a really good sniff. People tend to carry the most interesting smells on their purses, briefcases, or hands, which are a bit out of kitty's reach. By smelling those items thoroughly, your cat gets a good idea of where you've been, what you've done, and even if you've petted another cat (sacrilege!). Standing on their hind legs simply brings impatient kitty noses into good sniffing range.

Ah! cats are a mysterious kind of folk. There is more passing in their minds than we are aware of. It comes no doubt from their being too familiar with warlocks and witches.

Sir Walter Scott

It is said that a cat is always on the wrong side of a door—at least, cats seem to believe that. It's the nature of the beast to want what it doesn't have, and closed doors seem to be a personal challenge. Cats take patrolling their territory very seriously, whether that's inside the house, outdoors, or both. Doors simply get in the way. Cats don't necessarily cry to go use the rest room, they want to check the latest kitty bulletin board on the other side of that darn door!

folds, called false vocal cords, produce the purrs. Others believe a contraction of throat muscles is behind the rumblings. A third theory holds that purrs are produced by the turbulence of kitty's blood. Experts can't agree which is true, or if a fourth, unknown mechanism is behind the mystical purr. Only kitty knows how purring is achieved—perhaps one day he'll reveal his secret.

Kneading: As kittens nurse from their mother, their tiny paws rhythmically push and tread against mom's tummy. Kneading kitten paws massage mom cat's breasts to stimulate the release of milk. Later, adult cats often tread and knead with their paws when particularly contented, perhaps harkening back to their carefree kitten days.

5:00 Crazies: As the clock crawls toward afternoon, drowsy cats suddenly erupt. Vaulting from chair to floor, they dash madly about as though pursued by invisible fiends. Cats were designed to alternate naps with intense bursts of energy used to capture prey. Exuberant pet kitties without normal hunting outlets sometimes aren't able to contain their vitality. When they need to let off steam, they simply "explode" all over the house.

Potty Etiquette: A cat's toilet habits are a carry-over from the wild. Feral cats make their toilet far from the nest so predators can't follow the smell and find their kittens. Less dominant cats bury droppings to mask their presence in another's territory, while top cats leave feces uncovered as a reminder that they rule the roost. House cats may perceive people as the dominant force and cover their wastes in the litter box in deference.

Catnip Binge: Is catnip a feline aphrodisiac? Actually, the scent of this mint relative gives cats—even wild felines—a sensory high. The nerve stimulant affects a cat's brain, promoting relaxation and lowering inhibitions. Cats "on catnip" can act like frisky kittens, indulge in mating-type behaviors, or become lolling drunkards who drool and roll about like furry fools.

When owners move away, kitty may try to travel thousands of miles to return home. Homing cats read scent markings and visual landmarks that map their territory. They travel in wide circles to find familiar scents, sights, and sounds of a neighboring animal's territory that point to the right direction. Over longer distances, cats may rely on microscopic iron deposits in the brain that seem to react to the earth's magnetic field. But navigation ability varies, and some cats couldn't find their way out of a paper bag. Identification tags are the best device to ensure a wily wanderers' safe return.

LEGENDS

Ancient peoples unable to understand unique feline traits invented imaginative tales to explain them. Even today, feline legends are touching reminders of the mystery surrounding our cats.

Creation Stories: Medieval legend says the devil tried to mimic God and create a man; instead a sorry, skinless creature appeared—the first cat. St. Peter took pity on the pathetic beast and gave the cat her only priceless possession, a fur coat.

Another fable tells us Sun and Moon held a contest to see who could create the finest animal. Sun fashioned a lion and greatly impressed the other gods. Moon was filled with jealousy and created a sprightly cat. But the gods mocked Moon's imitation lion. Sun created a mouse as a sign of his contempt. Moon desperately tried again and created a monkey, but the monkey received even greater derision. Furious over her humiliation, Moon

This Turkish Van seems to be seeking high ground as if she's afraid to get her feet wet. However, these water babies never learned that cats are supposed to hate water. They are referred to as the Swimming Cats since they often like to take a dip in a pool. Turkish Van cats come by their love of water naturally. Born in the Lake Van region of southeast Turkey, these cats were often seen paddling about. The people of the region prefer their Van cats to have a distinctive shoulder spot. They call this the "thumbprint of Allah," indicating that the cat has been blessed from heaven.

His voice is tenderly discreet;
But let it be serene or vexed
Still always it is sonorous and profound,
This is his charm and his secret.

Charles Baudelaire

caused eternal strife to spring between the creatures. That's why even today, the lion hates the monkey, and the cat despises the mouse.

The Comely Cat: Legend also explains why certain cats look the way they do. It is said that the Manx lost her tail when Noah shut the door too soon and cut it off. Another story tells us Samson often swam the Irish Sea for exercise. One day as he passed the Isle of Man, he tangled with a swimming cat and nearly drowned. To get away, Samson chopped off the cat's tail, and the Manx has been tailless since.

The Tabby Cat: One of the most moving tales recounts the Madonna's tribute to the tabby cat. Baby Jesus was unable to sleep. His mother beseeched the stable animals for assistance, but none could help. Then a small, shy tabby cat stepped forward. After first thoroughly cleaning herself (so as not to offend the mother or her child), the striped gray kitten snuggled down beside Baby Jesus. Her rich purr filled the stable with a cat lullaby, and the baby fell asleep with a smile. The Madonna touched the kitten on her forehead in grateful benediction. From that day forward, all proper tabby cats wear an *M* on their brow in honor of the service they performed for the Madonna.

With one glance at this tabby cat, one can hardly doubt that her brow bears the Madonna's mark. In another part of the world, the M could easily stand for Mohammed, who was a great cat lover. The tabby cat bears another claim to fame. Some believe the first cat created was a tabby. According to folklore, Noah feared having lions on the ark. God answered Noah's prayer and caused the great cats to fall asleep. Soon Noah realized that the mouse was also a danger. Again Noah prayed for help; this time God caused the sleeping lion to sneeze and out sprang the world's first cat.

Although this beautiful Siamese has clear straight eyes and a perfect tail, earlier Siamese cats often had crossed eyes or kinked tails. Crossed eyes were explained by a legend stating that an ancestor stared too long and hard at Buddha's golden goblet. Another story tells how the Siamese tied a knot in her tail to remember something—which to this day she can't remember. Certain highly bred Siamese carry the "temple mark," two distinct darker smudges on their backs. The story goes that an unknown holy being once picked up a Siamese cat and left the shadow of his hands forever on its descendants.

Chapter 8

Cats in History & the Arts

"All right," said the Cat;
and this time it vanished quite slowly,
beginning with end of the tail,
and ending with the grin,
which remained some time after the rest of it had gone.
"Well! I've often seen a cat without a grin,"
thought Alice, "but a grin without a cat!
It's the most curious thing I ever saw in all my life!"

Lewis Carroll — excerpt from Alice in Wonderland

THEATER

Poetic motion, expressive voice, and a talent for the dramatic conspire to create in the cat a subject worthy of artistic celebration. Writers, artists, musicians, and the world's great minds often share their lives with cats purely for love.

Furry thespians often take center stage. Tchaikovsky's *Sleeping Beauty* ballet includes a beautiful *pas de deux* for two fairy-tale cat figures; and an opera was based on Balzac's *Loves of an English Cat*. The old story *Dick Whittington and His Cat* is a popular pantomime play starring a cat and is still presented to British children each Christmas. This play tells the tale of how Dick Whittington's cat, Puss, brought him fame and fortune.

Perhaps a cat just like this yellow tabby inspired the unique and engaging feline theatrical experience known as CATS. *No other theater production has touched the kitten within us like this Andrew Lloyd Webber musical. If not for a bit of kitty providence,* CATS *may not have been written. The T. S. Eliot verses upon which the production was based lacked a narrative thread. Then Eliot's widow gave Webber an unpublished, handwritten verse omitted from the original children's book. Called* Grizabella, the Glamour Cat, *the verse lent the production the central character it needed.*

The best known feline theater production is Andrew Lloyd Webber's musical *CATS*. With 36 feline characters, the show first pounced on stage in 1982, and 12 years later celebrated its 5,000th performance on Broadway.

The pantomime story of Dick Whittington and his cat has been told since the 15th century. Penniless Dick walked to London in search of fortune and ventured his sole valuable possession, his cat, in an investment scheme. When kitty sailed off with the trading vessel, Dick feared failure and started home. But on Highgate Hill he heard the bells of the city calling, "Turn again, Whittington, Lord Mayor of London." He returned and discovered the ship had traded on an island overrun with rats, which his cat had vanquished. Dick was rewarded with a princely sum. And in fact, a man named Dick Whittington did hold the office of Lord Mayor of London.

I could endure anything before but a cat, and now he's a cat to me.

William Shakespeare,
All's Well That Ends Well

ART & MUSIC

The earliest cat art was cave paintings, amulets, and sculptures, but later artistry illustrated real life as well as fable. Paintings on a Thebes tomb wall shows kitty retrieving birds for her master, while ancient Japanese works illustrate folk tales of vampire cats. The Japanese maneki-neko or beckoning cat figurine is a good luck symbol popular even today.

Painters like Leonardo da Vinci, Rembrandt, Rubens, and others included feline subjects in their works. Cats were also depicted in religious paintings. The first true cat artist was the 19th century painter Gottfried Mind. He was considered the "Raphael of cats" for his feline portraits. About 100 years ago, French graphic artist Théophile Alexandre Steinlen followed in Mind's pawsteps. His drawings of cats were seen all over Paris in advertisements and posters. The popularity of Steinlen's cat illustrations is as strong today as it was then.

This painting called Woman with Cat *is by Auguste Renoir. Cats often appeared as companions in the portraits of some painters, including the works of Renoir, Henri Rouseau, and Pierre Bonnard. But before them, Gottfried Mind (1767–1874) was the first to specialize in portraits of cats themselves rather than their owners. Mind always worked with his favorite cat nearby and with her kittens draped over his shoulder. In 1809, an outbreak of rabies resulted in the destruction of all cats in the city. Mind managed to hide and save his beloved cat Minette.*

The smallest feline is a masterpiece.
Leonardo da Vinci

Théophile Alexandre Steinlen (1859–1923) painted this 1898 work entitled Recumbent Cat. *Steinlen was a Swiss-born commercial artist who lived in Paris. He became famous for incorporating the cat in many of his advertisements. One of his poster advertisements for a tea company featured a mother and daughter sipping tea from large cups while a very large cat sat on the table next to the tea canister. Steinlen was so besotted with cats he couldn't bear to turn any away. His house in Paris became known as "Cats Corner."*

Modern times offer countless kitty calendars, posters, and greeting cards. From realistic renderings to cartoons and caricatures, there's feline artistry to satisfy the most demanding critic.

Music paints a distinct picture of the cat as does no other art form. Edward Lear's verse *The Owl and the Pussycat* was set to music by Stravinsky, and Rossini composed "Duetto Buffo Deii Due Gatti," a duet for two women singers who vocalize solely on the word *meow*. Cats have often appeared in popular music, too. The 1976 hit "The Year of the Cat" was a breakthrough song for singer Al Stewart. And who can forget Tom Jones singing "What's New, Pussycat?"

But perhaps the ultimate in feline music comes from cats themselves. When Domenico Scarlatti's cat ran over the piano keyboard, the composer immortalized the cat's paw-tread by incorporating the theme in a work he called "Cat Fugue." And when feline yodeling met modern technology, Mike Spalla produced "The Jingle Cats' Meowy Christmas," a collection of 20 yuletide favorites rendered by his cats. The debut album sold more than 115,000 copies and was followed by a second seasonal songfest, "Here Comes Santa Claws."

In 1871, Nonsense Songs *by Edward Lear included the engaging story-verse* The Owl and the Pussycat. *The work shown here illustrates the owl and pussycat setting out to sea "in a beautiful pea-green boat." When they marry, they "dance by the light of the moon." The story was a delightful inspiration for a musical work composed by Igor Stravinsky. Cats have inspired countless musicians. An opera by Hans Verner Henze was based on Balzac's* Loves of an English Cat. *Novelty songs like "Me-ow Song," written in 1919 by Harry D. Kerr and Mel B. Kaufman, poke fun at feline foibles.*

There are two means of refuge from the miseries of life: music and cats.

Albert Schweitzer

Artists around the world have been captivated by their feline subjects. In this painting entitled Cat on Windowsill *by 19th century artist Ando Hiroshige, a Japanese Bobtail kitty perches on a windowsill for the best view. Another Japanese artist, Tsuguharu Fujita (1886–1968), was a feline specialist who lived in Paris. Although he often painted detailed studies of cats by themselves, he included cats in self-portraits as well. Today, Ryozo Kohira is a contemporary Japanese painter who renders delightful works depicting cats acting like people as they steer boats, drink wine, and perform other decidedly uncat-like activities.*

Here, artist Salvador Dali shares his table at a book signing with his pet ocelot. Perhaps it is the untamed nature of this creator that is attracted to the seeming wildness of the feline. A number of artists have created works incorporating wild cats as well as domestic. Henri Rousseau painted a stormy jungle scene with a snarling tiger in 1891 called Surprise. *A series of cat studies by Leonardo da Vinci included more than 25 kitties with some evolving into lions. Practice sketches of kittens were made by da Vinci as a prelude to his painting,* Madonna and Child with a Cat.

LITERATURE

Cats purr and pounce through the pages of literature. Carl Sandburg's poem *Fog* captures the essence of the cat with "Fog comes on little cat feet . . .," and we are taught life lessons by cats in Aesop's Fables.

Despite his fondness for cats, Edgar Allen Poe chills us with the grim tale *The Black Cat*. We thrill to feline intelligence in Lillian Jackson Braun's *The Cat Who . . .* mysteries. This popular series features a newspaper reporter with two cats—one of whom is a crime-solving cat. Perhaps Ms. Braun's inspiration comes from her two Siamese cats. Nursery rhymes written by T. S. Eliot were published in 1939 as the *Old Possum's Book of Practical Cats*. The book is a valentine to the cats Eliot loved and is the basis for the enormously successful musical *CATS*.

This tabby cat belonged to Ernest Hemingway, who was an avid feline fan. His island home in Key West was shared with nearly 100 cats, many of whom had extra toes. Today, the Ernest Hemingway Home is a museum and shelter to the museum's current residents—50 felines, all descendants of the original six-toed wonders. Many authors kept favorite felines who inspired their writing. Edgar Allen Poe's tortoiseshell cat, Catarina, slept with the writer's sick wife to keep her warm. Charles Dickens's cat snuffed out candles with her paws when she wanted attention. More recently, Cleveland Amory wrote three books under the watchful eye of his white cat, Polar Bear.

It is the rare person who has not been touched by the magic of this man, Dr. Seuss, and his fabulous creations. Here the author is seen at the 1985 New York Toy Fair. The Cat in the Hat *children's stories have delighted even adults with their whimsical wisdom. Many engaging cat tales have been captured in literature for children. Beatrix Potter's* The Tale of Tom Kitten *and other feline narratives charmed us in our youth. Paul Gallico wrote memorable stories featuring cats, including* The Silent Miaow *and* The Three Lives of Thomasina.

The ancient story of Puss in Boots *is best known from the Charles Perrault fairy-tale collection but may have an Arabic or even Sanskrit origin. It recounts the tale of a young but poor man who gains wealth, a title, and the king's daughter as his bride with the aid of magical Puss's trickery. A host of make-believe cats have padded their delightful way through literature. Lewis Carroll's Wonderland stories feature Alice's cat Dinah, as well as the disappearing Cheshire Cat. Big cats roared into literature with C. S. Lewis's* The Lion, the Witch and the Wardrobe, *and A. A. Milne's character Tigger from his Pooh Bear stories has inspired generations of cat names.*

FILM

The first cat to appear on the silver screen was a gray stray named Pepper. She stole the hearts of silent film viewers when she starred with Charlie Chaplin, Fatty Arbuckle, and the Keystone Kops.

Some of the most memorable feline performances include those by Orangey, a tabby of that color. Orangey played the title role of Rhubarb in the 1951 story of a cat who inherited a million dollars. That same year, Orangey won the first Picture Animal Top Star Award (PATSY) for the role, which is the equivalent of an Oscar. Orangey also starred in and received the PATSY for the 1961 film *Breakfast at Tiffany's* with Audrey Hepburn.

In 1974, a four-year-old stray tabby landed the role of Tonto in the popular film *Harry and Tonto,* starring Art Carney. Usually allergic to cats, Art Carney had no problem working with Tonto, and a real friendship sprang up between the pair.

Dean Jones and Haley Mills starred with a Siamese in the 1965 Disney film That Darn Cat. *The feline actor, Syn Cat, played the part of D.C., which stood for dear cat or darn cat as the circumstances warranted. The cagey cat carried the key to rescuing a bank teller beneath his collar. D.C. was not the first acting job for this precocious kitty. Syn Cat costarred with two canine pals in the 1963 version of* The Incredible Journey, *playing the part of Tao. The trio traveled hundreds of miles to be reunited with their human family. The recent 1993 remake of this classic,* Homeward Bound, *starred a Himalayan named Tiki in the leading cat role.*

This is the crew of the spaceship featured in the science fiction thriller, Alien. Actress Sigourney Weaver holds the ship's cat, Jones, and the pair also starred in the sequel, Aliens. This orange tabby was one of two survivors of the alien's vicious attack. The cat actor playing Jones had a great role model in an earlier orange star, appropriately named Orangey. Orangey starred as Cat in Breakfast at Tiffany's, was Rhubarb in the film of the same name, and appeared in the 1962 Jackie Gleason movie, Gigot. Orangey won more show business awards than any other cat.

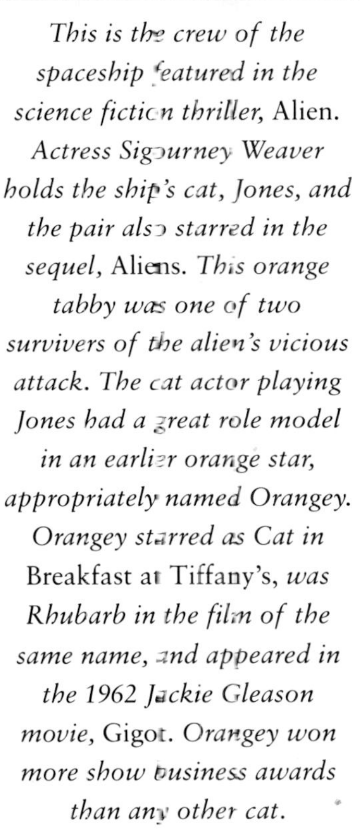

Puzzums the movie cat poses here with Maurice Chevalier. Nadine Dennis found and rescued Puzzums as a kitten, never dreaming she had a star on her hands. The cat was given a $250-a-week contract, which he signed with his own paw.

Kim Novak starred with a feline familiar named Pyewacket in the 1958 movie Bell, Book and Candle. This comedy told the story of a witch living in Manhattan who falls in love with a mortal. James Stewart and Jack Lemmon also starred, but it was the magical Siamese who won the film award for best "actor." He cast a spell on Novak as well, and the film's producer gave her Pyewacket to keep. Other cats have made a name for themselves in film as well. A Chinchilla Persian named Solomon was featured in two James Bond movies, You Only Live Twice and Diamonds Are Forever.

TELEVISION

Cats have been equally successful in television. A black cat named Midnight wore a diamond studded collar in the preview of each episode of *Mannix* and *Barnaby Jones*. A brown tabby named Burbank starred in *Frank's Place* with actor Tim Reid. Data's cat, Spot, on the popular series *Star Trek: The Next Generation* was first played by a Somali cat named Liberty Valance and more recently by two look-alike orange tabby cats named Brandy and Monster.

The Stephen King movie *Cat's Eye* needed several identical cats to play the part of General, but Burbank (of *Frank's Place* fame) and Floyd acted the lion's share of the role. Tyrone, a silver tabby, is best known as Toonces the Driving Cat on *Saturday Night Live*. But perhaps the greatest acting was done by a neutered male Persian called Maybe Baby when he played a mother in the USA Network thriller *Strays*.

This gorgeous, shaded silver Persian is the Fancy Feast Cat, well-known for his sophisticated, discriminating taste. The original Fancy Feast cat, SH III, is retired at sixteen and living the good life in Los Angeles, while look-alike Maybe Baby dons the great cat's mantle. Besides starring in countless television commercials and film roles, he has appeared in the television shows The Rockford Files, Dynasty, *and* Punky Brewster.

A cat is nobody's fool.

Heywood Broun

Above: *Taping a feline television commercial isn't all tuna and cream. This trainer is prompting the cat to perform the desired action using a buzzer or clicker device attached to a spoon filled with a cat food reward. Cats are quick to learn when they know what's expected. Felines with star quality must be able to repeat the performance until just the right "take" is obtained. Kitties learn to "hit the mark," touch a prop, and hiss or meow on command. One television star, Princess Kitty, will perform more than 70 tricks on command, including slam-dunking a cat-size basketball.*

Left: *No cat has been better known than Morris the 9-Lives Cat. Morris was 20 minutes from death when he was rescued from a shelter by animal trainer, Bob Martwick. The finicky feline became spokescat for 9-Lives Cat Food in 1969 and was soon the hottest actor around. He even starred with Burt Reynolds in the 1973 movie* Shamus. *He was grieved by many when he died in 1978. Martwick chose Morris' successor from another shelter. The new cat stepped right into the great cat's pawsteps and began working in 1979. He liked public life so much, Morris even ran for president in 1988.*

Just who is that distinguished cat in the black tuxedo? It's Socks, the First Cat, posed here guarding the front gate at the governor's mansion in Arkansas just prior to his move to Washington. After twelve "catless" years at the White House, Socks took the country by storm. Socks was given to President Bill Clinton's daughter Chelsea by one of her elementary school friends when he was just a kitten. Socks is the most recent feline in a long line of presidential cats. Abraham Lincoln had several cats and even rescued three orphan kittens during a visit to General Grant's camp during the Civil War.

Both the famous and the notorious have definite opinions about cats. Mohammed was very fond of a little cat he called Meuzza, and Anne Frank shared cramped quarters with a white-socked cat named Boche.

Hitler hated cats, perhaps for his inability to control them. Alexander the Great also despised cats, and Eisenhower gave standing orders that cats trespassing on White House grounds should be shot on sight. Napoleon was terrified of cats and was said to go into hysterics when faced by one.

Not every historical figure hated cats, though. Winston Churchill kept a succession of cats, including Nelson, Margate, and a marmalade cat named Jock. Woodrow Wilson had a cat named Puffins, and Calvin Coolidge kept three cats. More recently, Jimmy Carter's daughter, Amy, had a Siamese called Misty Malarky Ying Yang. The most famous political cat today is the First Cat, Socks, who has his own newsletter and fan club.

Numerous presidents have been fond of cats, including the 30th president of the United States, Calvin Coolidge. He had three cats named Timmie, Tiger, and Blacky. Tiger was a wanderer. One day when Tiger didn't come home, Coolidge asked a local radio station for help in locating his cat. The station broadcast Tiger's description and passed on the President's request to help find the cat. Tiger was discovered at the Navy building and returned to the grateful President. Timmie, shown here in Coolidge's arms, was the ultimate diplomat. He allowed the White House canary, Caruso, to strut up and down his back or even snuggle between his shoulders for a nap.

A number of Siamese cats have been housed in the White House. Rutherford B. Hayes's cat was the first Siamese cat to arrive in the United States. Here, Susan Ford, the daughter of former President Gerald Ford, poses with her beautiful Siamese named Shan. Another first daughter, Amy Carter, lived with a beloved Siamese kitty named Misty Malarky Ying Yang. Leaders in other countries have been enamored of the cat as well. Winston Churchill took his black cat, Nelson, with him in 1940 when he became Prime Minister of Great Britain. A chair was held for Nelson in the Cabinet next to Churchill.

PICTURE CREDITS:

Front cover: **Maria Pape/FPG International.**

Back cover: **Tetsu Yamazaki.**

Animals Animals: Anthony Bannister: 9 (left); E.R. Degginger: 152; Gerald Lacz: 42, 55, 59, 77, 125, 126, 127 (left), 128, 129 (top), 155; Robert Maier: 147; Patti Murray: 166; Robert Pearcy: 148 (left); Prenzel: 197; Renee Stockdale: 119, 153, 159, 193; Sydney Thomson: 122 (top); Barbara J. Wright: 192; **Archive Photos:** 211 (top right); AGIP: 207 (right); Orville Logan Snyder: 211 (bottom); **Art Resource:** 7, 13 (top), 14; National Museum of American Art, Washington, DC: 201; **Norvia Behling:** 149, 150 (top), 168; **Bettmann Archive:** 13 (bottom), 204, 209 (top), 215 (top); Jim Bourg Stringer: 214; **Chanan Photography:** 158 (left), 191, 194; **City of Bristol Museum and Art Gallery/Bridgeman Art Library, London:** 206; **Donna J. Coss:** 50; **Culver Pictures, Inc.:** 215 (bottom); **FPG International:** Leverett Bradley: 112, 171 (top), 179 (right); Rob Goldman: 137 (bottom); Larry Grant: 115; Steven W. Jones: 121; Thomas A. Moore: 171 (bottom); Jeffrey Myers: 138 (bottom right); Maria Pape: 181; Terry Qing: 135; G. Randall: 151; Jeffrey Sylvester: 131, 142, 165, 190; **Heinz Pet Products, 9-Lives Plus Cat Food:** 213 (bottom); **Richard R. Hewett/Shooting Star:** 213 (top); **Dorothy Holby:** 36, 44, 68, 73, 101, 127 (right), 132 (top), 133; **International Stock Photography:** John Bechtold: 141; Henry Mills: 136; **Larry Johnson:** 32, 185 (top); **Louvre, Paris/Bridgeman Art Library, London:** 14; **MGA/Photri, Inc.:** Thomas Firak: 117; Wally Hampton: 198; **Morris Animal Foundation:** 183; **Pat Ortega:** 8, 9 (right); **Petit Palais, Geneva/Bridgeman Art Library, London:** 205; **Photofest:** 210; **Photo/Nats, Inc.:** Paul Butler: 41, 85, 97, 144, 157, 167 (bottom), 177, 185 (bottom); Mary Clay: 170; Ann Reilly: 164; **Photri, Inc.:** 10, 113 (top), 122 (bottom), 129 (bottom), 158 (right); L. Cordero: 145 (bottom); Prenzel: 167 (top); **Private Collection/Bridgeman Art Library, London:** 207; **ProFiles West:** Peggy Daly: 132 (bottom); Tim Haske: 139; Peggy Koyle: 162; Phil Lauro: 116, 138 (left), 186, 195; Allen Russell: 138 (top right), 140, 150 (bottom); Ellen Skye: 118; Wiley/Wales: 179 (left); Bob Winsett: 123; **SuperStock:** 11, 19, 113 (bottom), 137 (top), 143, 145 (top), 154, 161, 163, 168, 174, 180, 189, 203, 209 (bottom); Victoria & Albert Museum, London: 15; **The Mark Twain House, Hartford, CT:** 182; **Tetsu Yamazaki:** Title page, 5, 6, 20, 21, 22, 23, 24, 25, 26, 27, 28, 29, 31, 33, 34, 35, 37, 38, 39, 43, 45, 46, 47, 48, 49, 51, 52, 53, 54, 56, 57, 60, 61, 62, 63, 64, 65, 67, 69, 70, 71, 72, 75, 76, 78, 79, 81, 82, 83, 86, 87, 88, 90, 91, 92, 93, 94, 95, 99, 100, 102, 103, 105, 106, 107, 108, 109, 111, 120, 148 (right), 169, 184, 199, 202, 208.